wet moon™

book 2:
unseen feet

written & illustrated by
Ross Campbell
Cleo's diary pages by Jessica Calderwood

design by Steven Birch @ Servo Graphics,
Ross Campbell & Keith Wood
edited by James Lucas Jones

Published by
Oni Press, Inc.
Joe Nozemack, *publisher*
Randal C. Jarrell, *managing editor*
Douglas E. Sherwood, *editorial assistant*

Oni Press, Inc.
1305 SE Martin Luther King Jr. Blvd.
Suite A
Portland, OR 97214

www.onipress.com
www.greenoblivion.com

First Edition: June 2006

ISBN: 978-1-932664-47-8

5 7 9 10 8 6 4

1. Bowden House
2. Vance House
3. Smith House
4. Westmiller House
5. Weitz Hall
6. Polsky Hall
7. Yardley Hall
8. Joseph Hall
9. Simmons Hall
10. Page Hall
11. Meyer Hall
12. Steve Hall
13. Burial Grounds
14. Head-Butt Video
15. House of Usher
16. Denny's
17. Marco's Diner
18. Lo Pan's
19. Swamp Things
20. Flower Power
21. Sundae Best
22. Lorelei Cemetery
23. Zurah Cemetery
24. Trilby's Apartment
25. The Boob Tube
26. Polly Poster
27. Everyday Is Halloween

28. The Lovedrop Residence
29. The Swanhilde Residence
30. Wet Moon High School
31. The Shoe Tree
32. The Bernarde Residence
33. The Zuzanny Residence

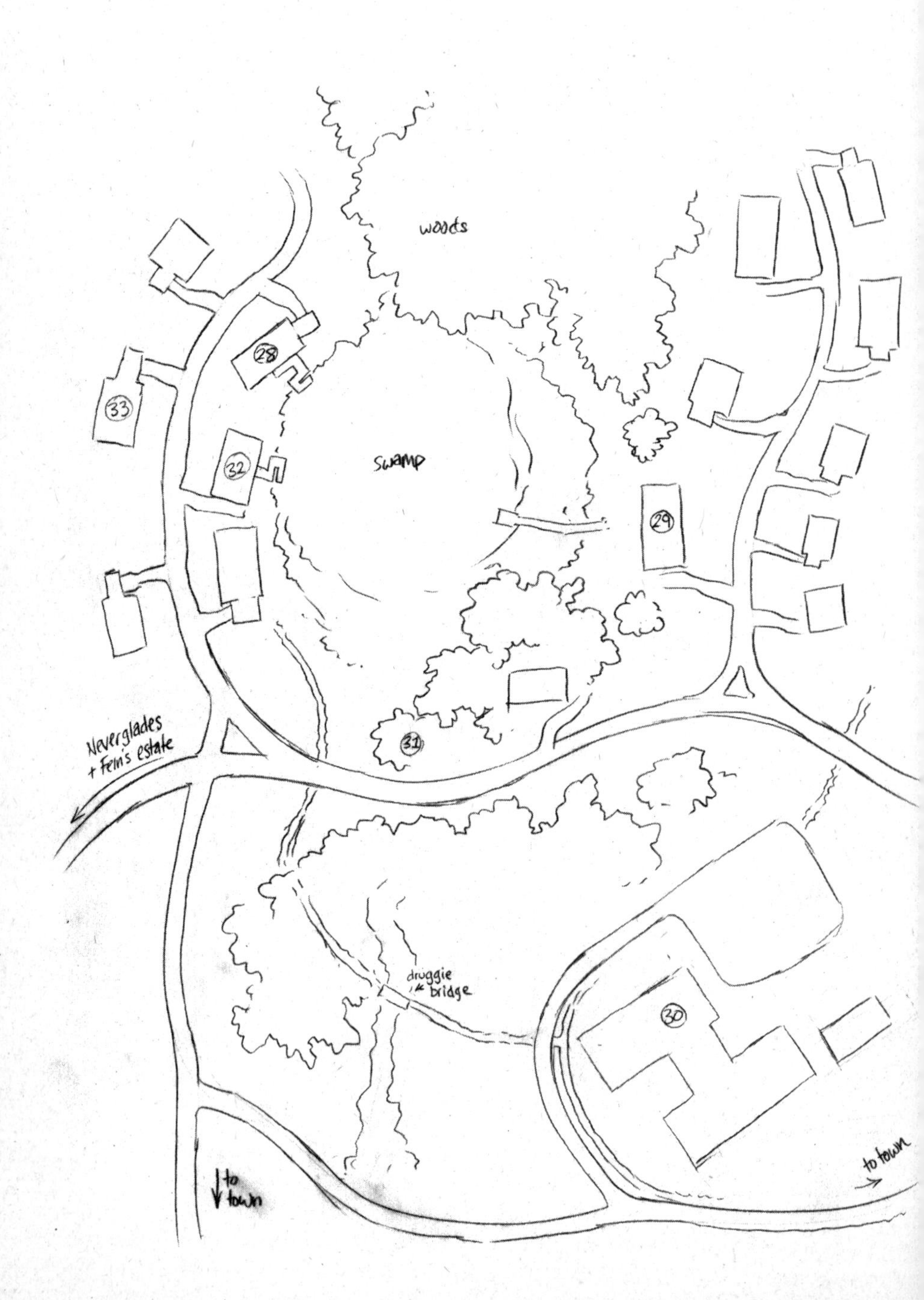

WET MOON HIGH SCHOOL
Okay, in y = sin x, the basic sine curve...
...appears once over an interval of 2π, right? So then in y = sin 2x, the sine curve appears **twice**...
...over an interval from zero to 2π... So, looking at this, can anyone tell me the **frequency** of the curve...?
HLETES!
ATH = AWESOME
Anyone? If the curve appears twice over an—
CleoLovedrop
Yes, Mara!
The frequency is 2 an' the period is π!
Ha, that's right! You're gettin' ahead of us!

SLIPKNOT
MARILYN MANSON
TRILBY = AWESOME
INTEGRATED
MODERN HISTORY
Hey!
Oh. Hey, Mara.

I gotta go to the office. Mr. Bride wants me, dunno why.
Uh oh, what'd you do this time?
I bet it's the shirt. Told ya.
Well... don't be nervous, it'll be fine. I'll wait for ya.
I dunno, who cares. Whatever.
I ain't fuckin' nervous. Jus' meet me by the vendin' machines. See ya.
Yeah, bye...
tak
tak
Oh, hi, Cleo! Here to see Mr. Bride, huh?
Yeah...
tak
tak
tak

You can go right on in, honey.
Yeah...
Mr. Bride...?
Come on in, Miss Lovedrop. Take a seat.
PAUL BRIDE
PRINCIPAL
So what is it?
Heh, you wanna get right to it, huh?
Whatever...

Okay, Cleo, well... I'm sure you know, but your... attire, is not appropriate, and I
Oh yeah?
PAUL BRIDE PRINCIPAL
Cleo, I **know** you know this by now.
EAT SHIT
So...
You can't wear this the rest of the day, okay?
stand up.
PAUL BRIDE PRINCIPAL
... same thing again? ...

Yes.
EAT SHIT

I'm completely outta everything now, I can't even buy anything faster than he can eat it!
Haha, I thought you just got a whole buncha burritos the other day...
I did!! He ate all **those** too, an' he keeps sayin' he'll replace 'em, but then he goes to the store—
an' he comes back with **cheese** burritos!
Heh, really? Does he **know** they're cheese? maybe he messed up.
Yes he knows, he totally knows. I bet if I didn't buy any food of my own, Slicer would totally starve. hmph.
Heh. what about the stuff he "replaces"?
Well, I don't think he'd have the motivation otherwise. I think he feels a slight, tiny pang of obligation or somethin', an' that's why he does it, I guess.
Except he's so... so, like, weird or whatever, so he jus' ends up gettin' stuff **he** likes.
Like a misguided husband buying his hapless wife a tool set for her birthday.
Yeah, 'cept I get none of the benefits.
Well, Trilby's making me eat all this vegan stuff now, so you should just come eat there.
She cooks some weird dish like every night...

Yeah, that sounds cool... Bet Slicer will freak out, wonderin' where I am...
Hey.
...Hi... You need some help there...?
Yeah. Sure.
Heh. I'll catch up with ya later.

what's in that box?
Secret. ...I've seen you before, you're Audrey, right?
Yeah, how'd you know?
Just heard it, I guess. I'm Kinzoku.
Oh, wow, that's pretty!
Well, hey, can I carry somethin' for ya?
Nah. I got it.
Oh, you sure?
Heh. It's not even heavy at all, I just pretended so you'd talk to me.
Oh...!

Hey, hon... where's Audrey at?
She went to put the moves on some girl in the hall...
Oh! The Asian girl from 'cross the hall? She's sooo pretty...
Yeah, she was Asian, weird tattoos...
She's got, like... this chain..? Like from her nose to her ear... I wish I had one...
Yeah, it'd be awesome, totally.
Heh, you think everything she does is awesome.
She could get, um, like some African lip plate and you'd like it.
That **would** be fuckin' awesome!!
She'd jus' think I was copyin' her, anyways, if I got one a them chains.
Shay juhs' thaynk Ah's copyin' her *innywahyys*, if'n Ah gots one a them **chayyns**...
Hyuk!
Shut ***uuppp!!***

That's what **you** sound like, not me! **You** talk like that more than me!
Haha, no way!
You said "them" chains. That's it, Cleo. That's it.
What the fuck're you talkin' about?!
Haha. Here, lemme wash your hair out.
No.
Okay, fine. Jus' leave the bleach on, then. Burn your scalp off. Fine with me.
Hmph. Fine.
Here we go, Martin...
...Cleo the bombshell comin' up!

Hey.

Hey, was wonderin' where you were...
Yeah, sorry. I ran into Connor again over by the Illustration building.
I hate having to go by there every time I fucking get outta class.
He's always lurkin' 'round over there, waitin' for ya?
Seriously... he's kinda starting to fucking freak me out, y'know? We like, weren't even dating...
I refuse to believe I was **that** good in bed to make him all insane now.
Natalie Ringtree quality was jus' too much for poor Connor, huh? You jus' too hot for your own good.
An' everyone else's, too.
He's just so **needy**, that's the problem. I hate dealing with people like that.
Yuck.

Like he's always asking me out for coffee, saying he's sorry over and over... yeah, he like, keeps saying sorry, but it's like... he wanted things like they were, y'know?
Like, all he wanted was a fuck-buddy, but now he's all weird, like he wanted us to be together all along.
Yeah.
Like, together-together, you know? I dunno. I don't know what to say to him now, except "go away."
So what you think about cleo so far?
Oh, she's cute, yeah... kinda bratty, though.
She reminds me of, um... a super-smart 8-year-old who's in college somehow. Heh. She's cool.
Yeah, a chain-smoking 8-year-old. I fucking hate the pillows-in-the-fridge thing, that has to stop.
You know what she takes all those pills for? She bi-polar or something?
No, um, it's like, somethin' with her heart. Like, it'll blow up if she doesn't take that stuff.

ORANGE
JUICE
ORANG
JUICE

SAWYER

ORANGE
JUICE

September 29th

last night I dreamed that I got up from my bed and went to the refridgerator, except it was like the refridgerator at Uncle Dwight's house, the gross green olive one, and when I opened it, there was this like giant jug of milk and not much else. So I decided I might as well drink it, and I drank the whole thing in one gulp. Then I got really scared, and ran back to my room, and that's when I woke up. Except I was sitting there with an empty carton of Natalie's orange juice in my hand. I really have to go out and get a replacement, and drink the same amount of juice that was missing before, so she won't notice.

I've started collecting every "Cleo eats it" flyer I find. So far, I have 7, which is about one every other day since Audrey found the first message in that bathroom. 6 of the ones I have were posted on paper, but the 7th one was written in marker on a window at Denny's, so I just recorded the time and place like the rest, since I couldn't take the window with me. I think the fact that it was written at Denny's must mean that whoever's doing this knows I go there, and knew I would see it. I still have no idea who it could be... I don't know anything about being an investigator.

Cleo Eats It:
#1: Simmons Hall bathroom - the first, found by Audrey
#2: outside Sundae Best - found by me.
#3: Weitz Hall lobby - found by Trilby.
#4: Corner of Magnara St. & Togo St - found by me
#5: Steve Hall lobby - found by Martin.
#6: Polsky Hall lobby - found by me.
#7: Burial Grounds peg board - found by Trilby
#8: outside House of Usher, found by Trilby
#9: Denny's window - found by me.

I can think of 2 possible suspects:
- Marissa: thinks I'm trashy. most likely hates me
- Trilby: i feel bad writing her here, but could it be she's just playing a joke on me? and pretending to be surprised by the messages? she's done jokes sort of like this before, so it's possible this is one of hers...
- my other idea is Natalie, she's been so cold to me since we met, but why would she write the messages before even meeting me? I doubt it's her. She seems too classy for something like this.

Ohhh god...
do you like it??
I dunnohhh...

Cleo. It looks **awe**some, honey, really.
Really...?
Yes. martin?

I really like it! It's, um... kinda punky or somethin'
Punky?? oh, nooo...

Cleo! Punky is **good.** You desperately ***needed*** punky.
hmph.

Cleo. It looks awesome.
I think I might miss the blue...
Know what Audrey said?
Haha. Uh oh.
I'm serious!
Okay, what **this** time?
Well... She said **Glen wants me**.
Ha, no way! How's **she** know?
I dunno, she said she can tell.

As much as I want this to be true, 'cause Glen is super cute, I don't think he wants you, hon.
What? Why not..?
Just as he is super cute, he is also super **gay.**
I'm surprised that **Audrey** didn't pick up on it, with her stupid ultra-gaydar.
Whaaat? He is not!
Cleo, he totally is. Okay, **may**be he isn't, but even **I** can tell.
I've never seen him with a girl before, or even a guy. Maybe he's asexual.
Ohh... he's so hot, though, I was all excited...
Aww... Maybe he isn't, then, an' you'll totally get it on.

yeah...
I think you should get with that Myrtle girl, myself...
Trilby, no.
Come on, why? She's super cute.
No.

Sure you're okay?

Yeah... I'm so sorry, are you okay? I always trip...
You were running pretty fast, too.
erasu

Yeah... shit.

I'm Myrtle.
Oh, um, I'm Cleo, pleased to meet you.
sure

I like it when I meet people by crashing into them.
It happens quite a lot, actually.
Really?

Sorta, yeah. Just last week, even, I met this other girl when she rode into me on her pedicab. The bike chain got all, like, stuck in my pants...
... so we sat there for like five hours getting it out. Then I got a free pedi-cab ride.
Oh... that's funny...
Yeah, heh. You wanna get some ice on that eye?
um, maybe...
It's lookin' kinda bruisy already. I felt a squish on my shoulder when we fell, bet that was your eye.
Yeah, I better... god, you think I'll get a black eye?? ohh...
era

ew...
I don't live too far from here, an' I got **loads** of ice...

I can't believe you live like **right** near me!
It's like, the same room, 'cept all flipped around!
Maybe my roommates are evil, bizarro versions of yours...
Ooh, are they home?
Nah... they're **never** home. But I'm sure not complainin'.

Oh! You like Mary Shelley??
Ah, my roommate Kaysa does, yeah... I started "Frankenstein" once, but I just couldn't get into it...

Aww, that's too bad... You should try "The Last Man," I love that one. It's about a plague...
Oh, cool. I like plagues more than undead monsters.
VOTE FOR PEDRO
erasure
Well... Frankenstein's Monster isn't undead, he's brought back to life...
He was dead, but now he's alive.
Hm, yeah... But isn't that what undead is..? Something back from the dead?
erasure
Um... I dunno... I think they gotta be, um, walking and dead at the same time.
Like a vampire or zombie. They're dead but they're up an' about.
Ah, I see. What about werewolves? You like them?
I guess so... not really. I don't like a lot of monster stuff.
That "Ginger Snaps" movie was cool, though.
Just Frankenstein, then? And, um... vampires?
Yeah. But Frankenstein is the doctor, not the monster.

DANZIG
Right, right. I knew that, actually. Okay, so, your eye is like, totally getting gross, um...
Yeah, stay there.
erasure
GRAVE-WORM

Oh no, I'm getting **gross**??
Booboo Bear!
TBM

DANZIG

Here he is! He makes having cuts and bruises fun!
erasure

Ohh, he's cute... what's he do?
Load him up with ice, then stick him on your face!
Thanks... I never seen a Booboo Bear before.
TBM
CRADLE OF FILTH
Well, this is the only one, actually.
Really..?
Heh heh, no, there's more than one... but this one is cooler. My mom made him, so it's a ton better than the store ones...
erasure
So there *is* only one!
The original store ones came first, but my mom, like, refused to buy one, so she made her own, except she coulda saved more time and money if she just bought one.
erasure

Well... I think that's real cool, that she made her own... she was bein' **creative.**
Yeah, somethin' like that...

cleo
eats
it

cleo eats it
DEO
BURIAL GROUNDS
BELLAMORTE
EVIL DEAD

Hi!
Yeah, hi, uh... I want, um... a large chai latte.
Sure, for here or to go?
To go, please.
$3.50.
sslurp
So this guy...
The... umm...
creeck
CHUD

cleo eats it
Oh, hey... hey, Beth, I thought you were off today...
No, tomorrow.
Who's this?
I'm Kinzoku, hi.
Hey. I'm Beth. What'll y'all have?
um... can I get, um... a medium Earl Grey...?
Yeah... $2.12.

EVIL DEAD

You should get coffee.
I always get tea... Jeez, Beth is so pissed at me.

Oh yeah?
Yeah. I been tryin' to get a date with her for like, ever, an' now... Now she sees me with you, and...
* sigh *
So?

Ah... I really **want** to go out with her, but it keeps gettin' messed up, an' now it looks like I blew her off.

So ask her. Right now.

I... I dunno, I don't think she wants to talk to me...

Just go, "Hey, Beth, 'member that date? How 'bout tonight, baby?"
Heh, I guess you're right...

While you're over there, see if you can get that one-armed girl's number for me.

7

What a mess
Always saying the wrong thing
Never listen
Here's to what I know...nothing
Fell into
Open arms of distraction
Unaware
Here's to what I know

- Autumn's Grey Solace

ÇADAVERIA
VOGUE

Heyyy, your hair!
Do you like it..?
I kinda miss the black, but this looks super hot.
Yeah, the black was cute ...

CADAVERIA
Hey, Cleo, you want some pie?
Ooh, what kind?
A7X
I got apple or blue-berry.
You had pie in your bag?
TSOL
I carry pie all the time, you knew that.
May I have a piece of both?
Well, whatever, I got a date.
Shit, you do? With who??

This guy, um... this guy Slicer, he's kinda—
No way! Slicer??
Yeah... you know him or some-thing..?
Yeah! He's my friend Audrey's room-mate! That is so weird!
Yeah, well, I gotta get ready, so...
you know this guy for real?
yes! he's such a gross jerk!
Nat seemed pretty weird about it...
wonder if she's embarrassed or somethin'...
yeah... i feel kinda bad now, i shouldn'ta said any-thing...
no, no, it's funny... Good pie, huh?

Yeah, it's real good... it tastes like... appleberry.
Oh god, check this out...
TSOL
cleo eats it
Check it ouuut. You really **are** famous, girl!
Oh nooo! Where'd you find it??
Over at Joseph Hall, the Painting building.
Y'think it was ***planted*** there for me to see??
Maybe... they do seem to show up in places me an' my friends go to...
How come you ain't doin' no like, super-spy investigation?
I don't know how...
SPECIMEN

You oughta get some superspy stuff, but that ain't necessary.
First, you gotta do a list of suspects...
I did that already... no good leads, though.
Ah. Um... Hmmmm... okayyy...
What abouuut... a stake-out?
What? What d'you mean?
Like... um, stakin' out a place, then you catch the mystery message monger red-handed!
...oh! Right! A **stake** out!! I thought- haha!
I thought you meant a **STEAK**-out, like the **food**!
god, I'm so dumb-
Heh, holy smokes, are you hungry or what?
hold on...
I think that's definitely the most annoying phone ring ever.
Teen VOGUE

Hello? ...oh, hi...! ...um, nothin', I guess... okay... yeah... 'kay, bye!
Who was that?
Oh, this girl Myrtle..? The one I crashed into, remember? She lives a couple halls down, like... over there.
Oh yeah, right. You hangin' out?
Yeah, I'm gonna go to her room later...
Your first non-roommate new friend! Oooh!

FUCK YOU
Hey— whoa, your hair!
You like it...?
Yeah, I love it... I think I might miss the blue, but... yeah, it's hot.
Thanks...
book of love
BIG TROUBLE IN LITTLE CHINA
Wow, you're even messier than I am!
Yeah?

Haha, shut up! It's actually **cleaner** than it was before!
Nice eye, heh heh.
Hmph. I can't believe it's not gone yet. Everyone thinks I got in a fight.
Or that my boyfriend hits me.
Maybe when it's gone, you'll have a cool eye scar.
Like a scar up and down across your eye, and the color part would be all white!
I prob'ly will, with my luck. I'll wear an eyepatch.

I think the only real scar I got is on my head...
It's under my hair, thank god...
Here, you can feel the bump, kinda...
Yeah... I can sorta feel it...
My best friend Trilby threw a math book at me in 6th grade.
There was one a those, like, protractor things in between the pages an' it stuck out an' gouged my head.
Heh heh, why'd she throw a book at you?
She didn't mean to, I don't think. It jus' slipped outta her hands when she was like, runnin' at me.
It was an accident. At least it didn't go through my skull.
Wanna see the best scars ever?
Sure... I think...?
They're actually the **worst** scars ever, but yeah, the best at being the worst.

You ready?
check it out.

Oh god!!!
Haha!

That—that's why
I took out all my earrings!!
I read about those!
I used to have my ears all pierced up, I dunno if it's an allergy thing, or...? I used to wear a big hat a lot, I think that made it worse.
I **told** Trilby about them, she didn't believe me!
Pretty grody, huh?
They... well, they aren't **that** bad...
I'll never have shorter hair than this, that's for damn sure.

... what about these ...?
Oh, I—
No, no, I'm sorry—shit.
Nah, it's cool. Really. I mean, whatever. Heh.
Sorry... I'm practically a stranger...

I'm sure you know where they're from, so, um...
Y-yeah... I used to, like... do that a little, but nothin' that ever left a scar.
Yeah... I been doin' it a long time... it's okay.
So... how come you were runnin' outta Weitz Hall so fast that one day?
Oh... this... this stupid guy... I'm so dumb, I shoulda known he'd be in that class...
SUPER METRO
Who?
This boy I used to date... Vincent.
Ooohoo, Vincent. He sounds dark and mysterious.
He is.

So... guess it musta been a shitty break-up, huh? If you're running away from him?
um...
Did he dump you on Valentine's Day? That'd be so bad.
But also kinda funny, if you think about it.
Yeah... I guess so. I was real in love with him.
It was a week afterwards. I was lucky. At least I got some Valentine flowers out of him before he dumped me.
sigh
Aw. Was this a long time ago?
Just a few months ago. In February.

Okay. It's almost October now, it's been like... five months, you gotta get out there, forget the gloom and get on the market!
Seven months.
Right! Seven! What did I say?

Five.
I meant get **back** on the market, not... just "get on." Get back on.

Yeah...

...Did you get to fuck him?
Excuse me?
Haha, sorry, that was mean.
Well, we made love if that's what you mean.
Yeah, that's what I meant... heh, sorry.
I've never done it with anyone.
Really?
Yep. Now you know one of my many dark, dark secrets. Guess I owed it to you.
Sorry I upset you with the fuck thing.
No... I'm not upset, it's okay...
You didn't have to tell me... I don't mind you're a virgin or whatever, it's not a dark secret. I think it's sweet. I wish I still was.
Now I feel kinda gross, sometimes, when I think about it.

Why? Was Vincent crap?
Oh, no, no, he was wonderful...
I get to hear about inadequate boyfriends all the time from Kaysa and Zia.
But... so how come you feel gross? Gross how?
Is it, like... a purity thing?
... A purity thing?
Yeah. Um, like... since you had sex with him, you don't feel "pure" any-more, know what I mean?
You- you gave something away to this guy, and he just shat all over it. Or you. Or whatever.
No... I've slept with a few other guys, so... I don't have a problem with that, but I do think virginity is important...
I guess I jus' woulda liked to give it to somebody who stuck around, an' I thought Vincent would.

Yeah... you think he came along just to bop you? Then that was that?
Guess so, yeah. We only had sex a few times... my friend Trilby says I'm easy.
All the other guys before Vincent were flings, I guess, even though I really liked them all. One didn't even tell me his name...
If, like... you don't wanna talk about this, or...
No, no, it's fine... Trilby never wants to hear it anymore, an' my friend Mara hates all men, an' my friend Audrey gets real mad about it, too. So it's nice to, like, get to talk to somebody else...
Heh. Your friends sound pretty rad.
So how'd you get dumped? E-mail? Heh heh.

No, thank god. I don't even got a computer. But, um, no, it was a pretty normal break-up, I guess.
He called me up, like, tellin' me to meet him in the park for a walk, which was a little unusual, so I thought it was some special afternoon date...

so i got all dressed up... an' i had a blue rose i was gonna give him...
... i thought this would be the perfect time.

an' when i tippy-toed up to kiss him...

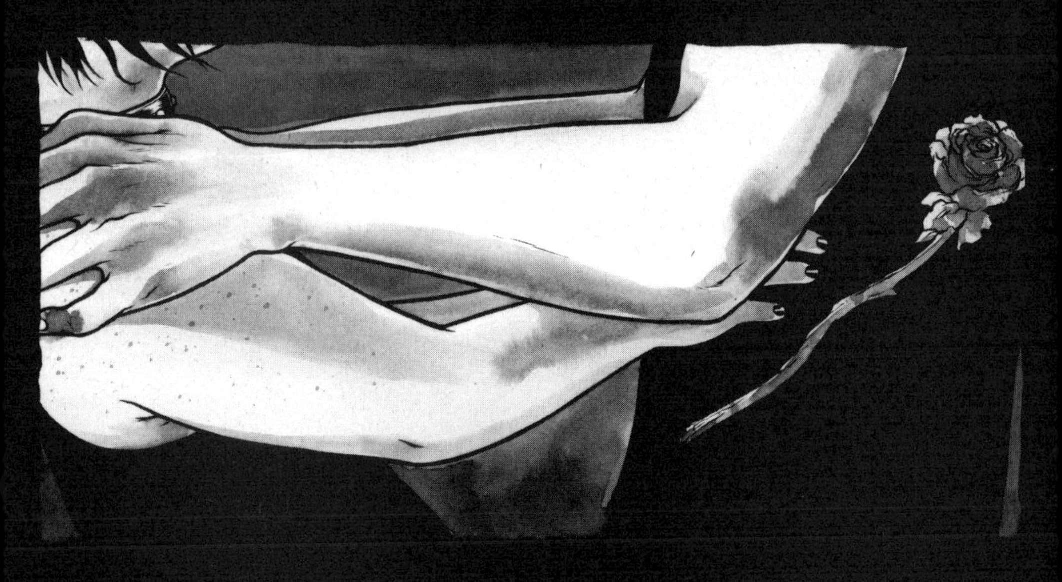

he shoved me away.

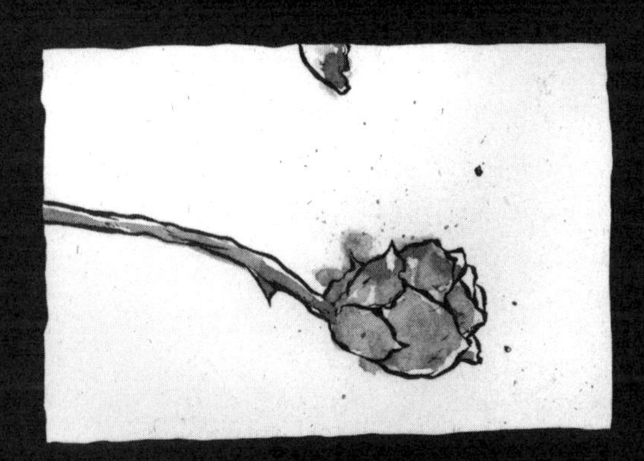

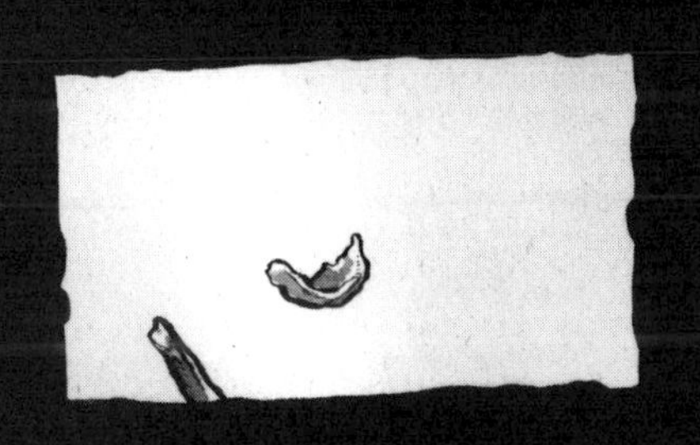

i tried to talk to him or whatever, but he... all he said was that he came to tell me it was over.
when he left, he even stepped on the rose. i still don't know if he didn't notice or if he did it on purpose.

Penny??
Yeah, I'm up here, dad!
Hey, how come you're home?
Oh, I jus' couldn't get any **work** done at my place...
They're doin' all this construction out-side, I can't **stand** it.
Heh heh. So how's it goin'? Haven't seen you in a while!
I knowww, sorry... I've been real-busy with all this Fern stuff, that's all.
How's that goin'? She's the one with the mansion?
Yeah. She's payin' me a whole lot, since I'm doin' pretty much her entire house!
That's great, Pen. How—
ding donnngg
Oh, crap, I'll get it. It's Dale.

Hey, Mara. What is it?
Cleo here?
No. She's not at the dorms?
No, obviously. I don't know where she is, thought she might be here.
Well, she isn't. Sorry.
God. You're such a fuckin' snot. Thanks anyways.
What the fuck, Mara. What's your fuckin' problem, anyhow?
See ya.

cunt.

ugh. Cleo. where the fuck **is** she?

... so that's why I always run away from him.

That's pretty intense.
Yeah... I can't face him.

That's rough.
Yeah...
So what about that class? You gonna drop it?
I haven't even showed up since that first day, they prob'ly failed me for so many absences.
I feel so bad, too, the professor, he looked so... like, when I walked in, he seemed so hopeful about me bein' in his class.
He was kinda cute, too.
Haha. what'd he look like?
Um... glasses, kinda scrawny for an older guy... messy hair...
It's Mr. Kreysig! I got him for my Satire class! He is kinda cute, you're right.
You should switch into my satire class!
Yeah, maybe I will...

He introduced me to this FBI agent the other day, isn't that nuts?
Wow, are they friends?
Yeah. Like... who the hell's friends with an FBI agent? They don't have friends!
Mulder 'n' Scully never had any outside the FBI, neither did Dale Cooper.
Wonder if he'd figure out the "Cleo eats it" thing...
I bet he would. For all we know, that's **why** he's here in Wet Moon.
Was he cute? I think all FBI agents have to be attractive. Like Mulder, Scully, Agent Cooper...
Kiefer Sutherland an' that singer guy from the "Twin Peaks" movie...
You like 'Twin Peaks'?
Some of it I like, yeah.
Yeah, I do!
That singer is Chris Isaak. You think Kiefer Sutherland is hot?
He was so yummy in 'Lost Boys' an' 'Stand By Me.'
Haha, he was in 'Stand By Me'?
He was the lead bully!

Wait, he... oh wait, yeah! I totally remember that! Yeah, guess he wasn't bad in that...
He's the best in "Lost Boys." I love vampire bikers.
Heh. Since there are many other things featuring vampire bikers.
No, well... you're right... but there're enough of 'em in that movie, though.
So you're really into mullets, huh? Heh heh.
No! I jus'... like biker guys, I guess, that's all... Kiefer Sutherland can wear a mullet all he wants, that's fine by me.
I sorta had one when I was like, five or something. I'd totally grow one again.
You could do like... a mohawk mullet. A mullet-hawk.
Yeah!

Maybe it's time for something totally new.
Wonder if an FBI agent would go out with me.
I could get Agent Wolfe's number, I bet.
Ooh, is that his name?
Heh, yeah. Agent David Wolfe. Such a great FBI name. He has a monkey, too.
It like, sits on his shoulder and goes like, nyow! nyow!
Shut up! He has a **monkey**? I've totally seen him!
Haha, really? Where?
In Denny's! He sits there with his monkey!

Haha, whoa! He brings the monkey into Denny's? Can he do that? Ha.
Yeah! They sit there an' eat pie! He's kinda hot, but I bet he's too old for me.
He looks, like... what, mid-thirties?
Yeah, prob'ly. That's not too bad... I could be with a 30-somethin' guy...
BIG TROUBLE IN LITTLE CHINA
Oh, I was gonna ask you... um, you know Glen...?
Heh, yeah, I work with him.
No, I know, I mean... you think, like... he's gay?
Yep.
Oh... you think so...?

I **know** so. You don't think it's obvious anyway?
I... yeah, I guess... So, like, he told you or whatever...? That he's gay...?
Well, sorta... Like, I thought it was obvious but I wanted to make sure, so I casually asked if he was dating anyone, and he said sort of, so I asked "what's he like?"
I just tossed that "he" in there, kinda casual, you know, and so Glen told me all about some guy.

Oh... 'cause, um... my friend Audrey told me Glen was into me, or like, she thought she could tell he was, anyway...
Audrey's always real good at like, tellin' if a guy's gay or not... Guess not this time.

Isn't he so hot, though?
He's okay, yeah.
You don't think he's cute...?
Um, I do, I guess... He's got a cute smile, but he's not really my type...
Most obnoxious ring ever.
book
Hello..?
Hi! ...No... No, I'm at Myrtle's... Myrtle. Yes.
What— I thought you were out with Martin... well, I— why don't— Trilby, come on over, it's room 454...
Yes, what's your problem?! 'Cause I thought you were out, silly, that's why!
Well, fine, don't! She— no, I'm not! I am not! Goodbye!

Trilby, huh?
Hmph. **Yes.**
She...rrgh, I hate when she gets like that! Like, she went out with her boyfriend Martin, who's real cute an' sweet...
...but she totally blows me off to hang out with him, an' before I came over here when we was doin' my hair, she up an' left with Martin outta nowheres, an' now I'm here with you an' Tril's all mad I'm not home! **And** she calls me a **dyke**!
I told her to come here an' hang out with us, but she said no.
I can't jus'... wait around for her all the time like I guess she wants me to.
f love
She makes me so **mad** sometimes. I need a smoke.
Ew. Okay.

book of love
well, sorry.
An American
SILVER BULLET
THE FLY
Ginger Snaps
DOGSOLDIERS
WOLF
SUPERMAN
RABID
UNDERWORLD
CURSED
WRONG TURN
GARBAGE PAIL KIDS
FRIGHTMARE
DEMONS
ESCALATOR
HE-RA
RINCESS
OF
OWER
book

Who you like better: Beth, or that Kinzoku girl?
Hmm... well, Kinzoku definitely has a cooler name, but Beth has better hair. But Beth's tattoos aren't as cool as Kinzoku's... And what's with the nose chain?
What is she, from the 90s or something?
But that's also cool at the same time... but it isn't as cool as Beth's chopper.
I dunno... I don't even know if Kinzoku is *in*terested, y'know? I can't figure her out...
You just ***met*** her, nobody figures anyone out that quick. Is Beth like, *really really* mad?
I think so. She didn't say much, but I can tell.
Hey, is that Cleo over there? Look at her hair!
Oh, wow.
Hey! Cleo!

Hi!! whatchy'all doin' here?
I ran into Glen here outside, he was a little confused, heh.
This is what you were doin' to your hair??
I thought your room was 223! In which dwelled a little girl and a guy who looked like Vin Diesel.
the Slutty Angels
Nooo, 423!
Cleo, I swear you said 223.
'Least I finally found you, I almost didn't recognize you! I can't believe you went blonde!
Yeah... d-do you like it?
Yeah, it's cute! I love the back... but I think I might miss the blue, haha.
I'm used to it already! I love that you cut it all short!

I still can't decide if I like it or not...
So what're you doing over here?
I'm hangin' out with Myrtle!
the Slutty Angels
Oh, cool! Wow, I can't believe your black eye is still there!
I know, do I look completely awful?
No, no! It's going away, you look great.
Seriously, sweetie, it's almost gone. It looks kinda sexy, anyways.
Hmph. That's what Tril says, too. She said I look like a thug.
chk
I don't think you're allowed to be a thug if you're scared of birds.
What?! Do you remember that seagull that like, attacked me??
My sister got hit by a seagull once.
See??

So scary.
God I hate birds.
How 'bout penguins?
Well... I guess they're okay...
You told me you thought kiwis were cute.
Fine, them too.
And you like **cooked** birds, too, haha.

Yeah! I eat chicken an' turkey 'cause I *hate* chickens an' turkeys.

So where's Myrtle?
Oh, she's inside... she was kinda disgusted when I said I had to go smoke.
Aw.
She said "ew." She sure knows how to make me feel bad.
I doubt she meant it like that, Cleo.
Hmph. I dunno... I can't believe she didn't even come out here with me.
Even if somebody doesn't smoke, they should still keep the smoker company...
I think Myrtle's just against that stuff, that's all.
Against what?
Like, against smoking or whatever.
Well... that doesn't mean she should be mean to me jus' 'cause I smoke.
Is she straight-edge or somethin'?
Shh, guys, talk quieter.

Hm, I dunno, not sure...
Still... she could at least come out with me...

Hey, guys...
Hey, Myrtle!
Where'd you come from, Glen?

Nowhere, just hangin' out. You know Audrey, right?
Yeah, I do. She comes into Head Butt all the time, duh.

Well, now it's official: Myrtle, this is Audrey. Audrey, Myrtle.
Nice to really meet you, finally.

Yeah, you too...

Anyone wanna go downtown with me? I gotta see if my Mary Stuart Masterson poster is in yet.

STOP

CANN AL
CORP SE
SZZHZZHM

OUT 9 IN 0% FLOATER 1 TIME

RIDDICK
THE LITTLE MERMAID
LAND OF THE DEAD
SPIRITED AWAY
NEW X MEN
THE ABANDONED
You think Myrtle seemed... kinda pissed or somethin'...?
Yeah, definitely a little weird.
I know! Everything was great 'til I went outside... she was real cool...
Aww. You **like** her, hmm?
Whata you mean **like** her?
Hehheh. I'm jus' jokin', Cleo. She never did the change-hand-touch on you, so...
Why y'all think– Rrgh! Nevermind!
Still not in.
You shoulda called ahead!
Naah... I like coming down here, y'know? It's a nice walk.
the Slutty Angels
Yeah, an' you can find weird stuff like this psychedelic Godzilla poster!
Look, he's all cute an' cartoony!

I think that's Polish.
See, we never woulda found this otherwise!
the Slutty Angels
the Slutty Angels
Whoa, look at this girl...
I think her name's Zia, she takes photos of herself like, on the ground and all covered in dirt and garbage.
Wow!
She's so cool...!
I wonder what happened to her arm...
She works with Beth at Burial Grounds ...

Seems kinda silly...
I haven't seen Heroin Girl in a few days...
Hope she's not dead some-where.
I saw her yesterday, over by Swamp Things. She's alive an' well, don't worry.
Maybe alive, but definitely not well.

8

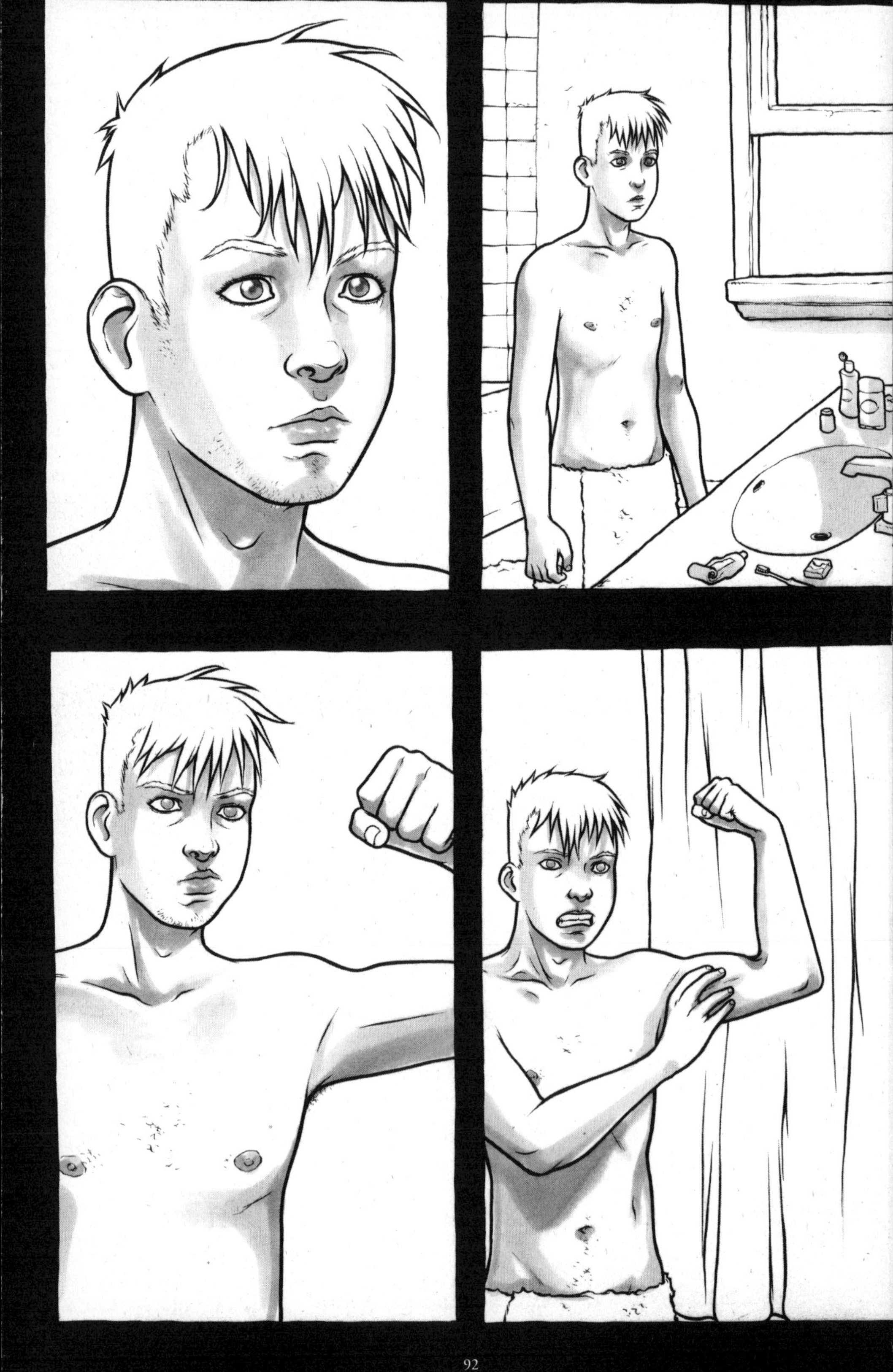

KNOK KNOK
You almost done in there? Jeez.
Yeah... hold on.
Gotta get spruced up for your **woman**, eh? Hehheh.
I'll be out in a minute.

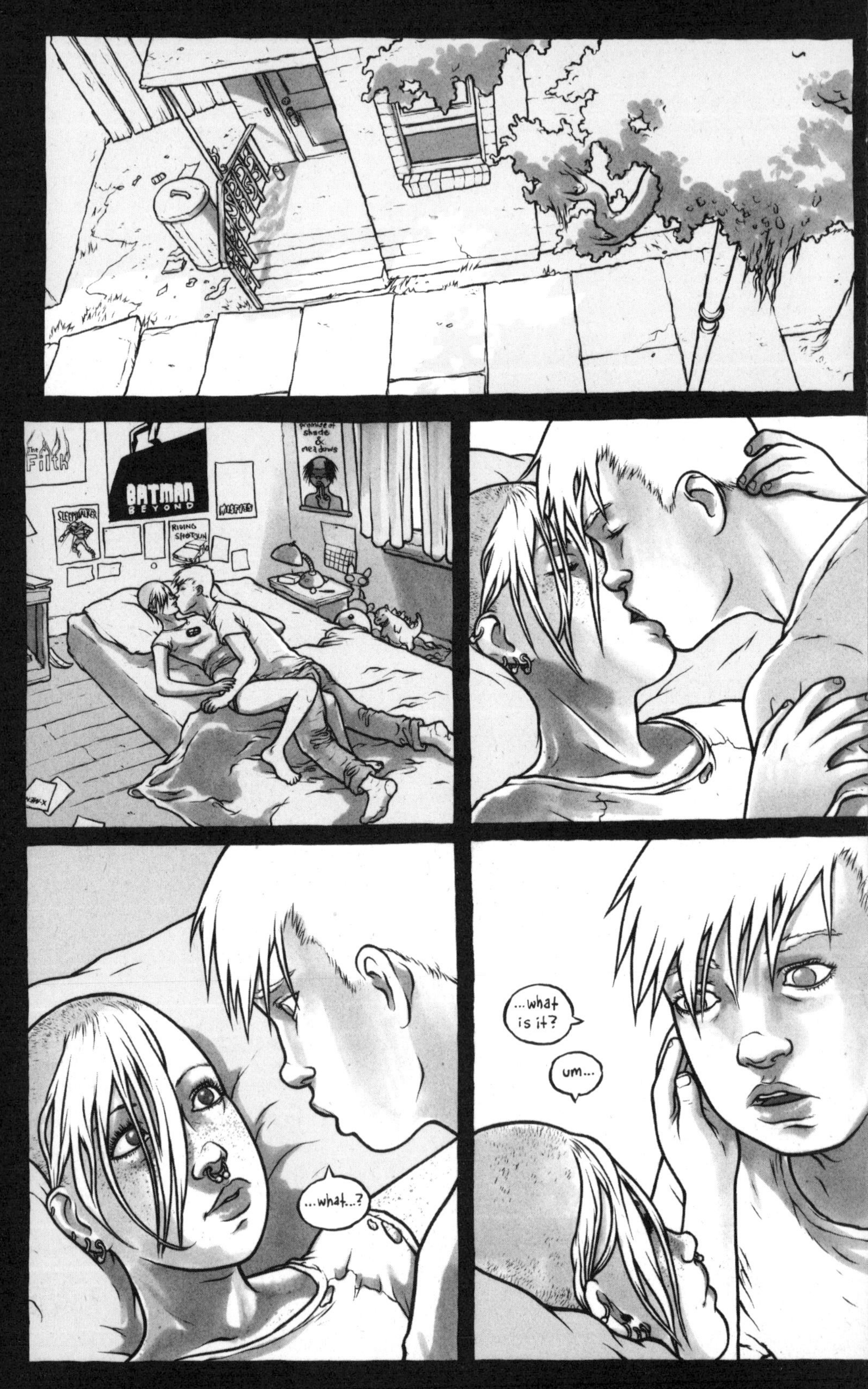
The Filth
BATMAN BEYOND
SLEEPWALKER
RIDING SHOTGUN
MISFITS
promise of shade & meadows
...what..?
...what is it?
um...

Wh-what d'you mean...?
Like... your hands, you don't... you're not doin' nothin' with 'em, y'know? I'm sayin' you could do somethin' with 'em...
Y'know... you can, like... you can use your hands, if you want...
That... that could be cool.
Yeah... sorry...
Don't be sorry, jus'... yeah, I'm jus' sayin', is all.

Okay... you need some help, or...?
No, no, I don't...
So...
...what now?
um...
No rush...
Oh-!
fup

I like that.
5:23
Okay... now what?
Um...
Okay...

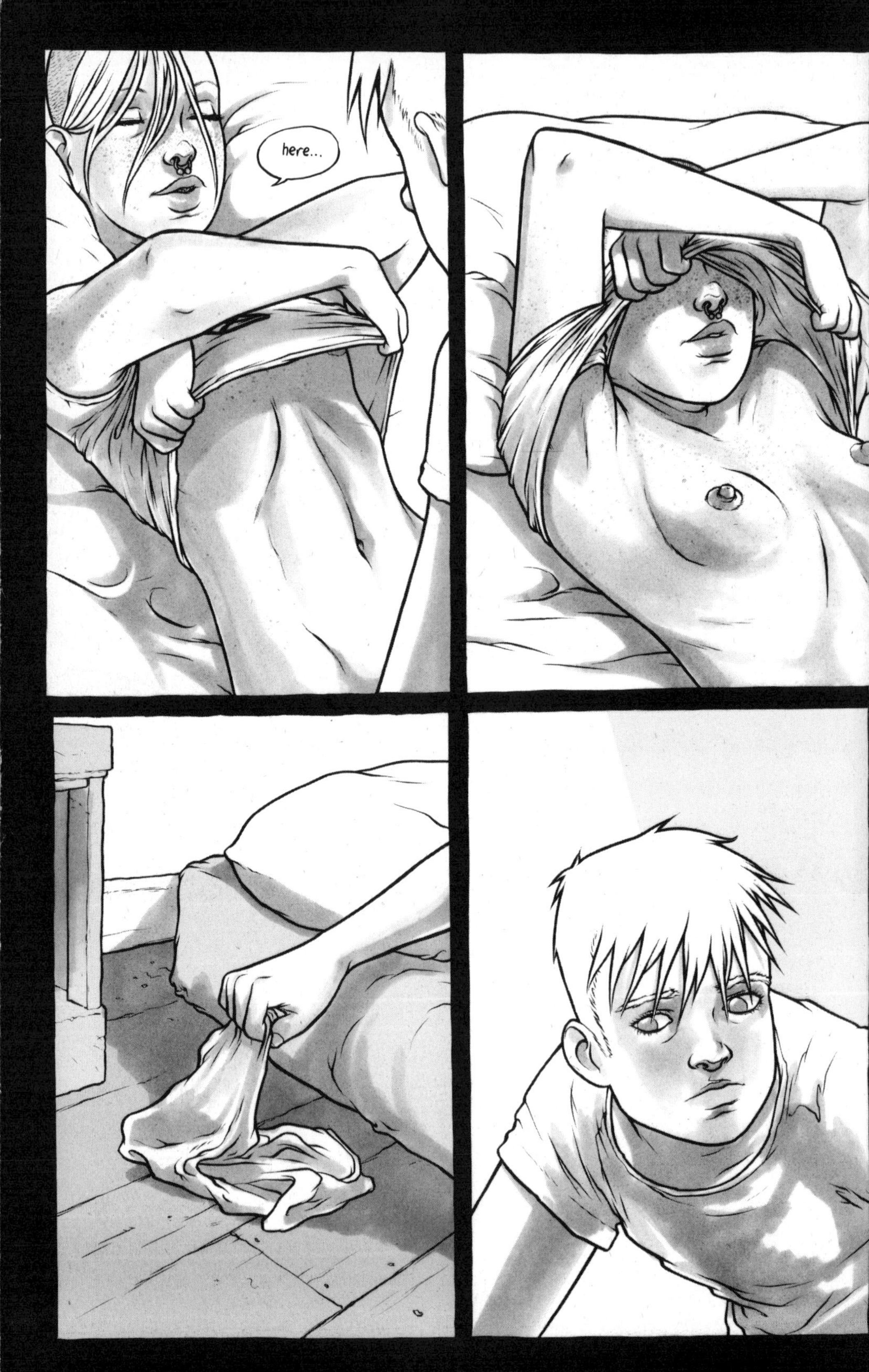
here...

yeah...
you okay, hon?

Oh my god. So Natalie has a date with Slicer! I forgot to tell you!
Oh god, are you serious?
Completely serious. I wonder where they met...
Maybe now he'll spend time at your place an' eat all your food! Ha!
No, he'll eat everything! My yogurt an' my leaf cookies an' Malady's pie...
Cleo! Leaf cookies?? What about your diet?
Ohh, jus' leave me alone... I thought we were talkin' about Slicer!
It's okay to cave, Cleo.
I didn't— I didn't cave... fine, okay, so I ate some cookies! Who cares!
Don't tell Tril, you'll never hear the end of it!
Does this mean now you'll eat Reese's Pieces?

God, you guys, I hate group projects, I got the dumbest group ever.
Oh, for your survey class?
Yeah.
whatever. I dunno. Dumb diet wasn't workin' anyways. I'm gonna eat so much shit now an' I don't even care.
Survey of what?
Greek Art. How come I'm always the one doin' all the work? Everyone else jus' goofs off!
You can't tell the teacher?
Well—oh my god, this one ugly girl in my group, she, heh heh, everyone calls her E.T.—
What, E.T. like the alien?
Yes, god, ain't that the meanest thing ever?
Heh heh, yet you're smiling.
It *is* funny, but **I** don't call her that, I jus' call her Ellen, so—
Oh god, what an awful name, too. Poor E.T.
the Slutty Angels

So this **girl**, right, last class I was wearin' that yellow top, the one you like, Cleo...
Yeah! The cute one!
So, I had that on, an' I go to sit down, an' the E.T. comes ov
Hey, there's Mara!
Cleo! what the fuck!

But, so
Oh my god, what'd you **do** to your **hair**?!
You don't like it...?
Well, it... I liked the black, the blonde makes you look like... a whore or somethin'.

Thanks. Mara...
Where were you, anyways? I been fuckin' everywhere an' you're nowhere!
Ohh, I'm sorry... I was hangin' out with that girl Myrtle an' she
The black eye girl?
Well... yeah, but it wasn't on purpose, though, and...
Yeah. So you hangin' out with her?
Hi, Mara.
the Slutty Angels
Hi, Glen.
BURIAL GROUNDS

I don't think I can come here anymore if she's here.
Jus' talk to her. She's sweet, hon.
I knowww... she's sweet, but... she ain't very... understanding.
Look at Glen. I can't believe you thought he was straight.
Okay, okay. Sorry. So he's gay 'cause he's talkin' to a guy?
the Slutty Angels
I can't believe you thought he was straight, Cleo.
Well, Cleo, sorry I got your hopes up.

The spider skirt.
It's okay...
There's this cool guy in my Poetry class, anyway. I think he was lookin' at me last time, so tomorrow I'm gonna wear somethin' cute. Not sure what, though...
This is remarkably optimistic of you, Cleo. I'm proud of you.
Gimme a break.
Aw, thanks! I had a real great weekly horoscope on Monday, so I think my luck with boys is gonna change with this one.
Hopefully he got a thing for black eyes.

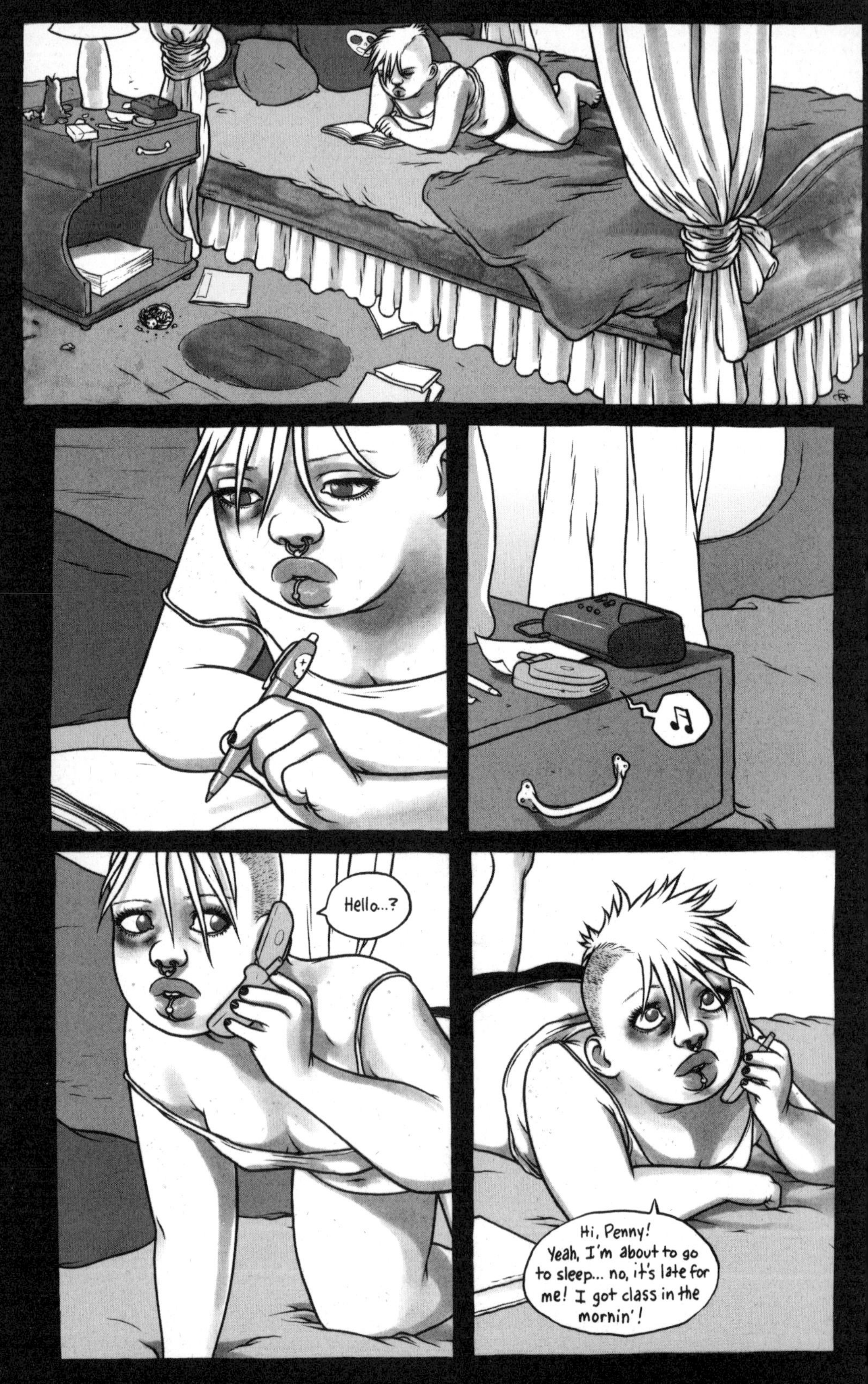
Hello...?
Hi, Penny! Yeah, I'm about to go to sleep... no, it's late for me! I got class in the mornin'!

Oh, okay, that's cool... I'm at home right now, I got Meiko next to me... I know, hehheh.
...No, they're cuttin' down trees outside my place, I can**not** stand it.
purr
So how are you?
I'm good... I called for two things, actually. The first one is I found somethin' you're lookin' for.
What is it??
A few pages from your book.
Nooo! I mean yes! You found them! You didn't read 'em, did you??
Please don't read anything!!
Well, I kinda read some, yeah. Is that bad?

Ohhh goddd, why'd you **read** them?? You **know** you're not supposed to! I told you **not** to!!
It ain't a big deal, who fuckin' cares? So I read like, two pages outta, what, like three **hundred**?
No, I know... thanks... but you shouldn'ta read 'em!
Cleo, I found your fuckin' lost pages, you should **thank** me!
Ohhhhh gawwwwdd
ANYways, the OTHER reason I'm callin' is to invite you over to **Fern's** tomorrow night...
What?? Fern's? Why?? I—
She says she wants to meet you, but there's actually a secret reason why I want you to go.
A-a secret reason ...?

Yes. A week or so ago, she asked me about you an' said she saw a photo of you in my purse—
Ohh, you got a picture of me in your purse?? You're so sweet, Penny, I—
Cleo! Listen, come on!
So anyway. Fern. She said she saw you at that Usher club, an' that she remembered you from this photo I apparently had in my purse. ...
But I am positive I didn't show it to her.
So... you think...?
She must've gone through my shit, that's all I can think of.
Oh god, you really think so...? I don't think she did that...
She had to, how else did she see it?
I guess, but... she seems so sweet...
So that's why I want you to come, to investigate.
Cleo, you wanted to meet her, this is your chance!
Ohhh, no, I can't do that!
I... I got this black eye still, I can't—

I'm not... a spy or nothin', I dunno how to snoop...
Cleo, that's dumb. Your eye is fine. C'mon, I want you to meet Fern.
You are the ultimate snooper. You an' Trilby both. C'mon, Fern wants to meet you anyway.
But... she's so nice, I wanna be friends with her, not... not, like, spy on her...
Could we do it after me an' her are friends...?
That is so dumb. Fine, don't come with me. I dunno what I'll tell Fern.
Well... I guess I could go... okay...

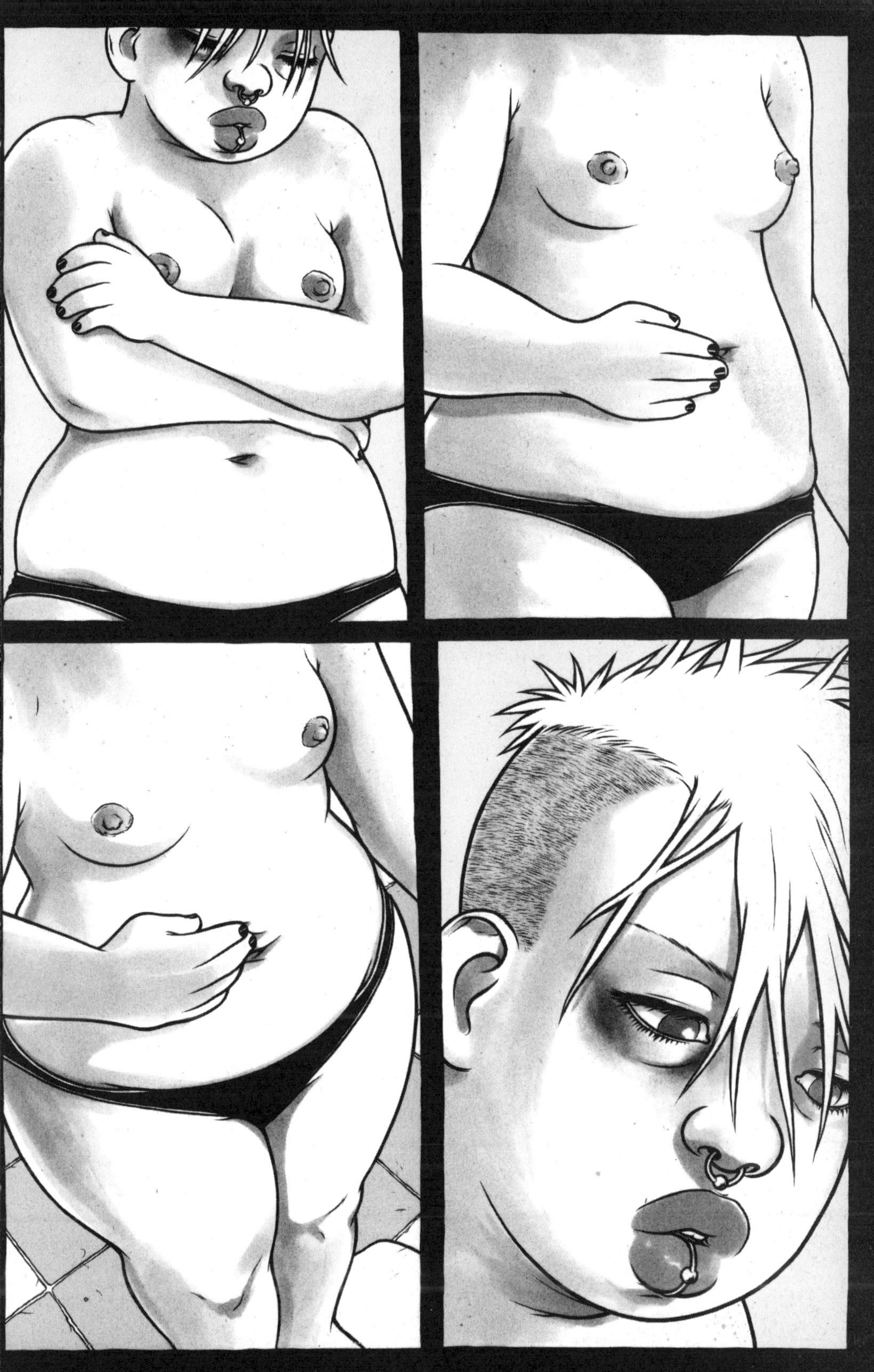

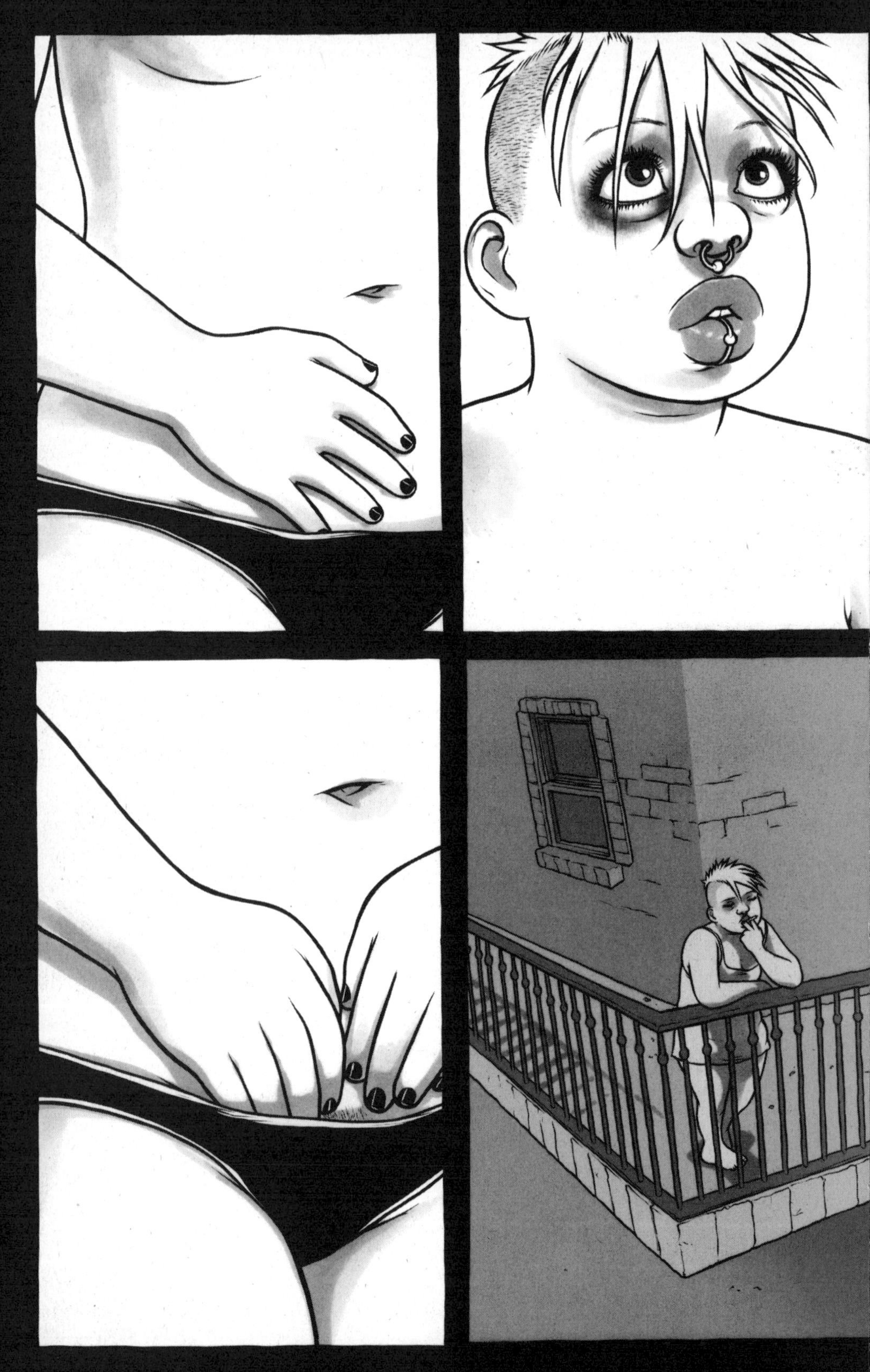

haha

stop it! I said I hate that stupid mask! take it off!
blugguhg ggghhghg! haha!

oh my god, I do not want to see that! ew! haha!
grab me another drink while you're in there.

Oh, hi kitty... where'd you come from?

How'd you get all the way up here? Do you live up here?

hey... you are very cute, yes you are...
spsspsspss... kitty kitty kitty... it's okay, i'm nice...
good kitty...
Ow!!
ow... bad kitty...

KNOCK
KNOCK
hello...?

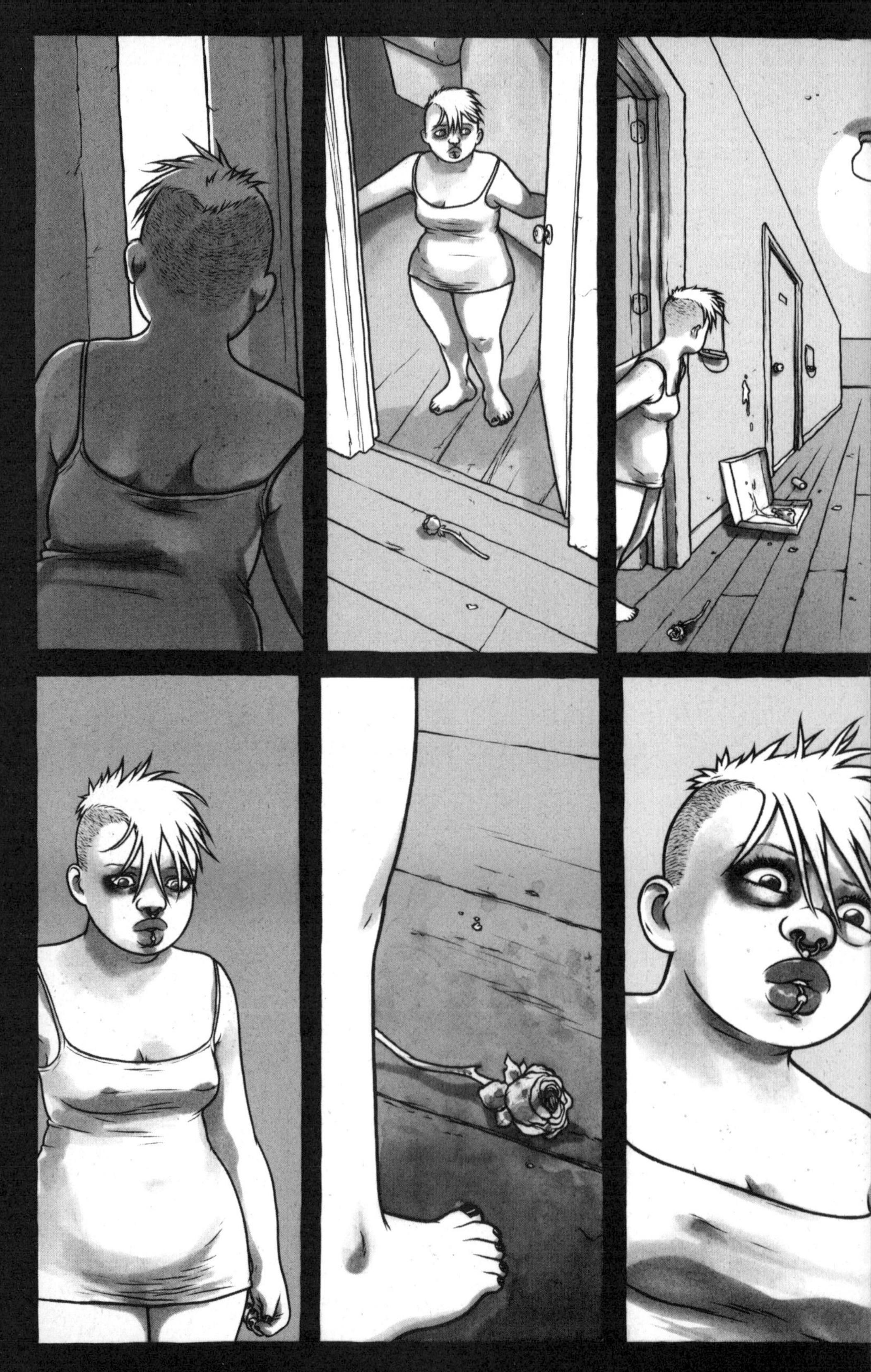

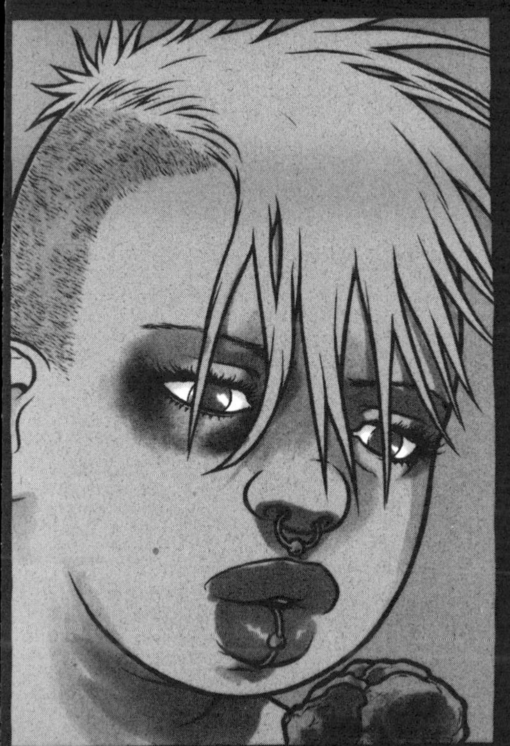

September 30th

I don't think anyone likes my new hair. I'm starting to regret letting Trilby convince me to go blonde... I guess I like it, but I'm already sick of everyone saying they liked my old hair better. Maybe I should just dye it back to black again.

But more pressing is this rose I just got outside my door! Who could've left it? There are only two possibilities, I think: Myrtle, or Vincent himself. God, I know I shouldn't feel this way, but would I really be glad if it was Vincent? Why would he ever do this? I feel like I'm weird about this, so I can look at myself and know that I'm being stupid when I'm hoping it's Vincent. We have no future. I don't know why, but he hated me and he wanted to hurt me. He still hates me, I know it. I sort of wish I hadn't told Myrtle what happened with the break-up. She's really cool, but... it just feels too soon. The whole thing still feels like it happened a week ago rather than months.

I feel like Myrtle knows everything, even beyond the break-up. I feel like by telling her what I did, I've opened up these doors, and now she can just look in and see everything else that's still in there.

The rose has to be from Myrtle. It's not Vincent, it can't be him. Maybe Myrtle really does want to go out with me, like Trilby keeps getting at... I don't think I could be with a girl, though. Especially ones I've only known for a couple weeks. And she does the hand-touch thing to Audrey all the time at the video store, but she's never done it to me. The 2 times she rung me up last week, there wasn't even a hint of it. She probably doesn't even want to touch me at all.

I better go to bed. I didn't mention this before, but I think I've arranged pretty foolproof routes to each of my classes this semester, which will help me avoid Vincent. I figured out what other classes he has, so that I could plan my routes accordingly. I have to get up a little earlier in the morning, since it takes me longer to walk to class, but it's a small, small price to pay. I've prepared a super-cute outfit for tomorrow, which includes my spider pocket skirt and black t-shirt with the cleavage hole (which shows off just the right amount of what little cleavage I have).

9

Darkness comes like fear into the waiting world tonight
I watch the full moon gather through the black clouds in the sky
Another dim-lit room with staring shadows all around
I sit and wait for them to change with bloodshed on my mind

- Bella Morte

Yeah, come on over. Yeah, I'll be here.
Heh, **yes**, Cleo. I'm here right now, sittin' outside in my pj's, so jus' come over.
Okay. I'll be there soon... 'kay, bye.

NATE AND STEVE
RIDING SHOTGUN
See? Told ya I'd be here, you dummy!
So what's up? How was class? You seem pretty mopey.
Yeah... I wore my spider skirt jus' for this one guy in my dumb class...
...but he was really into this other girl with awesome boobs.
Aww, the spider skirt, I was gonna say... there had to be a special occasion.

I never get to see you anymore.
What? What're you talkin' about?
I... you're always with Martin, you never call me any-more.
Cleo, I've only been with Martin for like... not even two weeks, an' that's not long enough to be "always" or "never."
Right? Come on, hon...
How come... how come I don't get to hang out with you two..? I thought we were gettin' tattoos, but...
Cleooo, things're jus' startin' out with Martin, it's how it is in the beginning... An' we'll get tattoos this week-end, okay? We'll be so hot for that Bella Morte show!
Yeah...
There's somethin' else, right...?

... sorta... yeah...
You are the worst hider ever. I could so tell.
I don't... I don't wanna say it. It's so stupid, an' you'll get real mad.
I'm not gonna get mad, Cleo.
Yes you will. I know it.
I won't.
Yeah you will...
Lemme guess first, then...
ummmm...
You blew it on your diet.

That's it, huh? Ha. I'm not mad, Cleo, I don't give a shit. I knew you'd cave.
No, well, I mean... I did blow the diet, but that wasn't it...
You gotta lay off the burgers an' grease an' shit, not jus' sugar..
But okay, I'm gonna say it... You can't get mad, 'member?
Right.
Audrey told me you told her you an' I, uh... messed around that night we went to Usher last time. Like... we did it.
Oh god, see?? You're mad!!
Wait, she actually **said** that **I** said that?!
Nonono, well, she said... like, she said you ***implied*** it... then she jus' figured that...
But... I guess that... I wish you woulda said somethin' to ***me***...
I been worryin' about it this whole time...

God! Audrey! She's got such a big fuckin' mouth!
I'm totally callin' her on it next time I see her. Boy oh boy.
Trilbyyy, nooo, please don't...?
Gah. Whatever.
How come you didn't wanna talk to me about it?
I dunno, it was stupid, I was... drunk or whatever.
I wasn't even sure if you thought I remembered any of it, so I jus' left it alone.
Who cares. Let's jus' forget it.
Okay. Forgotten.
Okay... I guess... yeah...

So how're things with Myrtle?
What, you say that like we're goin' out.
I'm jus' askin' how—
Good, yeah, she's real cool...
But guess what somebody left at my door last night: A blue rose.
Whoa, really? Like in the hall, or outside your bedroom?
Hallway. I was all about ready to go to sleep, when there was a knock, but when I opened the door, nobody was there.
Cooool... Who d'you think it was?
I dunno...
Uh oh, is your Vinsense tinglin'?
Maybe...
I think it might be Myrtle, I told her the break-up story yesterday, so... yeah...
Who else knew about that rose? Y'think somebody's playin' a joke on you...?

Haha, oh wow, she's totally into you!!
I think that's actually real sweet, Cleo.
...yeah, it is... I know...
She's definitely a dyke, too.
Trilby! Come on...
So obvious.
I predict y'all're gonna be hot 'n' heavy innn... a week. Maybe two.
Nuh uh.
We should totally do a sleep-over tonight! Maybe Myrtle will show up!
Or if it's not her, we'll nab the rose-dropper in the act!

Yeah!
maybe Martin could help, too.
Yeah... that'd be cool...
So you— oh, wait! I won't be back 'til later tonight...
What? How come?
I'm goin' to Fern's with Penny.
Whoa! Really?? Man, can I come?? Fuck the mystery item-dropper!
Oh, sure... I'm sure it'll be okay. I should call Penny jus' to make sure, though.
She thinks Fern snooped in her purse, so I'm s'posed to like, spy or investigate or... or somethin'.

Sweet!
We don't gotta fuck the item-dropper though, we won't be there that late.
We can do a sleepover after-wards.
Awesome. So much ***intrigue*** all of a sudden!
I'll call Audrey an' Mara, too.
Oh yeah, you gotta see my new comic!!
Oh, cool!

THE CRAZIES
HOOKED ON CRACK
SWAMP THING
THE CROW
DAWN OF THE DEAD
LAND OF THE DEAD
SCANNERS
POD PEOPLE
RIDDICK
X2
SLITHER
X-MEN
MAD MAX
THE SPECIALS
FANTASTIC FOUR
Here it is! You're gonna love it.
Heh heh, jus' read it.
Haha! Oh my god, is this—

NIGHT FALLS...
AND SO I RISE...
...TO FIGHT!

HEY BABY, NICE NIGHT, EH?
GET HER PURSE!
TO REPAY MY DEBT TO THE LIVING, MORTAL WORLD, I FIGHT AS ITS CHAMPION!
LEAVE ME ALONE!!
SHUT UP, BITCH!
SOME-BODY HEL-MMMF!
NOW WE GET DOWN TO BUSINESS, HEH HEH!
UNGGH!
SCREAM AND YOU'RE DEAD, BITCH!

UNHAND HER, MORTAL, IF YOU WISH TO LIVE.
WHO—?! WHO THE HELL YOU THINK YOU ARE, MAN?!
GET HIM!!
SLASH
AAAGHH!!

ZZ-
ZZOOK
SHLUK
GO! TAKE YOUR MONEY, MORTAL!
WH-WHO ARE YOU ...?
...I AM
NIGHTDEMON

So?? What d'ya think?? 'Member Night-demon??
He turns his hand into a drill...?
Haha, yeah! I gotta show 'em to Connor! Haha!
But... you're obviously makin' fun of him, Connor's not **that** dumb...
Oh come on, it's an **homage**! Haha! Nightdemon!
SWAMP THING
Hahaha! Take your money, mortal!!
Well... I'm not sure I **get** it, but... I really love the art, though, it's your best stuff.

What's not to get?? He's this demon guy who's tryin' to reform so he has to help people!
An' he can turn his hands into drills! Ha ha!
Yeah... I like it. It's real good.
Whatever. You jus' don't know how to appreciate this kinda stuff. It's **ironic**.
Well, um... I guess I jus' like your zombie kitty comics better...
This is only a brief departure. I'm gonna do a CadaverCat/ Nightdemon crossover where they fight, too.
Why do they gotta fight?
I dunno, it's funny. 'Cause like... superheroes always have like, crossover fights... y'know...
No, I get it, but... Cata... CadaverCat's not a superhero, he's just a kitty...
Cleo, jeez, you're readin' too much into it! It's jus' s'posed to be stupid!
Sorry...
Jeez.

clink

plip

10

October 1st

I can't believe I'm going over to Fern's house in just a few hours. I've been thinking about what I should wear all day. I thought about my spider pocket skirt, but Trilby would make fun of me for wearing it again in the same day. And I feel like it's been soiled after it went to waste on that stupid boy in my 20th Century Poetry class this morning. How could I have even thought he was looking at me? I have a black eye, crappy blonde hair, no boobs, and I look like a boy. I don't care anymore. He was probably just staring at my eye. It's started turning kind of greenish-yellow now. Fuck that stupid boy and his monstrously-breasted girlfriend (since I'm sure they're dating now). But she is really beautiful. I can't blame the guy for liking her. Oh well.

Maybe if I had my old hair, though, he would've at least paid attention... everyone else seems really unimpressed or even spiteful with the blonde. Oh god. How can I go to Fern's with this hair?

Everyone else hates it, and I just know she will too. She's like beautiful darkness incarnate, gentle shadows given flesh... blonde is the antithesis of everything Fern! Why am I still writing this?? I know what I have to do!

423
PINK DRESS
I should totally grow a rat-tail.
Hey, sorry —
NOOOOO! What'd you DO?!?
I dyed my hair...

Everybody hated the blonde, okay?
Who cares?! You should care what I think! An' I think the blonde is hot!
425
Fern woulda hated it.
How do you know? She could be real into blonde, you don't know that!
Yes I do.
Do not.
Do too.
Well, fine. You'll regret it.
I guess you're jus' too daaark for blonde hair, right? At least you spiked it up...
'Member in 4th grade when your hair was all grown out?
You were like, twenty times darker back then, an' you were blonde then. It's totally dark enough for Fern.
I'd be more worried about your friggin' eye.
It's not that— it— I jus' don't wanna be blonde right now, okay?
Okay, well, you're denyin' your true color, then.
Your hair yearns to be blonde.
cleo eats it

Well, then your hair doesn't wanna be pink anymore!
Whatever, my hair wants to be pink.
How do you know mine wants to be blonde?! Maybe it's ashamed of its blatural non-Rrgh! I mean natural-natural blondeness!!
Hahahaha hahaha!
Rrrgh! Shut up! You KNOW what I meant!! I— shut up!!!
HAHA HAHAHAHA HAHAHA HAHAAA HAA!!!
I'm totally growin' a rat-tail.
Y'all got new 'do's, I gotta do somethin' new, too.
Wouldn't a rat-tail be hot?

Heh. Maybe I'll grow a tat-rail instea
Shut up! Like you never switch letters! You're the one who's always like, "oh, I'm so dyslexic!"
What the fuck you talkin' about? That's a joke about Marissa, re-member?! Jeez. Memory-Girl!

Okay, guys, give it a rest. Y'all better behave in there!

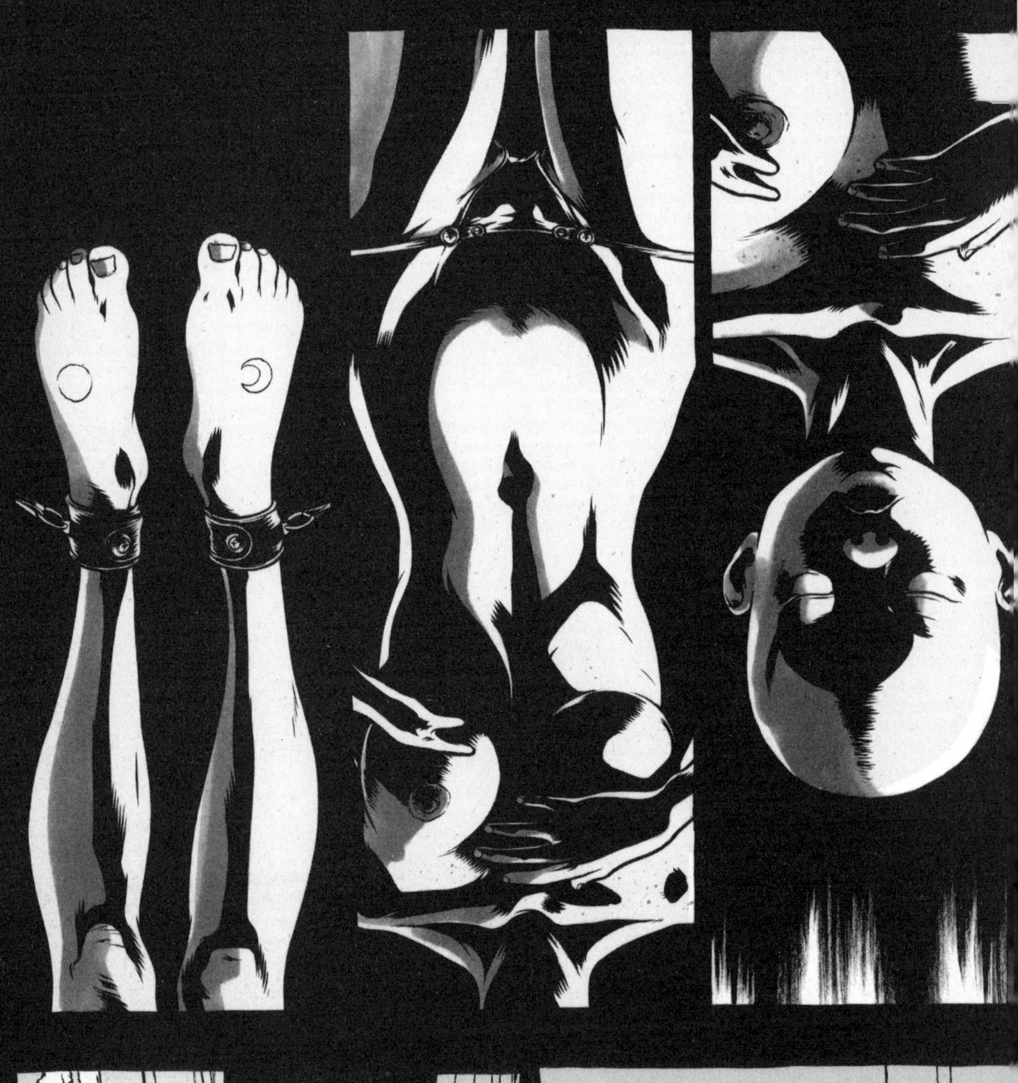

Hi, Glaucus.
Good evening, ladies. Come in.
Miss Fern will be joining you in just a few moments.
That's fine, she can take her time.

So what're we lookin' for, here?
I dunno...
...anything weird, I guess. Yeah.
Look, Fern caught Jaws.
Maybe if Fern lets us sleep over some time, we can sleep in rooms like this!
My room's cooler than this.
Can you imagine a sleepover with Fern? Like at your place?
Heh, yeah, like playin' Darkstalkers an' shit, watchin' dumb girly movies.

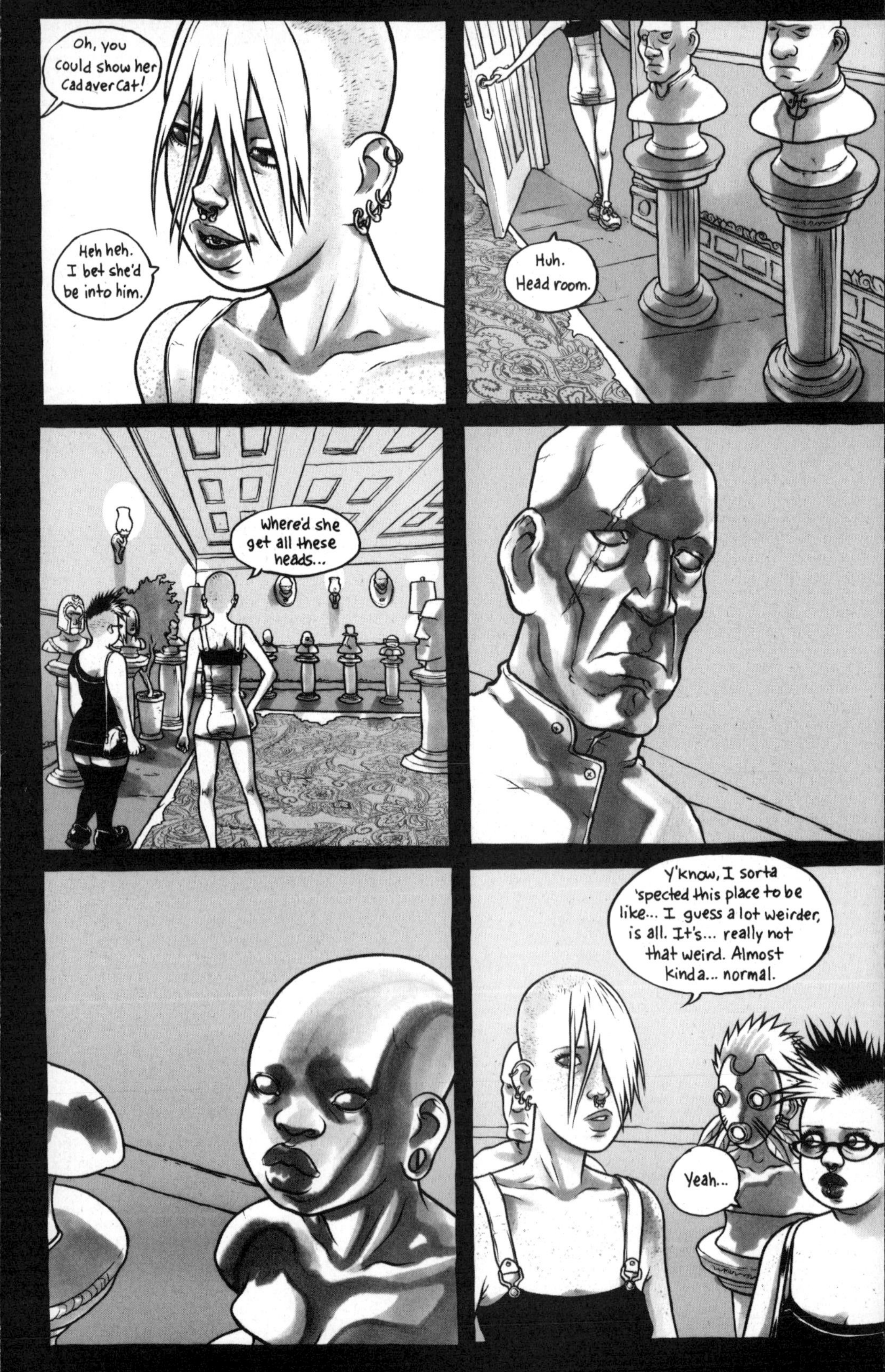
Oh, you could show her CadaverCat!
Heh heh. I bet she'd be into him.
Huh. Head room.
Where'd she get all these heads...
Y'know, I sorta 'spected this place to be like... I guess a lot weirder, is all. It's... really not that weird. Almost kinda... normal.
Yeah...

We ain't gonna find whatever Penny wants us to find, neither. What're we even lookin' for?

shit...
what?

I forgot my pills, I think... shit...
who cares, we won't be here that long.
I know, but I kinda forgot to take them earlier, so...

I figured I'd take 'em here...
Heh. Well, jus' don't get too excited.

I guess they're jus' explorin', they'll be back soon. I told them where we'd be.
that's fine... sorry you had to come out here in this weather.

Ah, it's only a little rainy.
It's weird bein' here when like, it's not **business**... It's nice.
I like this one! It's so small an' modern next to all the other bathrooms.
Look at this!
Whoa! Skull soap!
What's this doubletub all about?
Looks new.
Maybe, um... so two lovers can— well, no, lovers would wanna be in the **same** tub...
Where the hell're all the secret passages?

there you are! i thought maybe you'd gotten lost...
oh...!
i'm happy to finally meet you, Cleo.
Pleased to meet you, too, Fern... This is my best friend, Trilby...
nice to meet you, Trilby. would you two like anything to eat or drink?
my chef made some amazing peach pie today...
Ooh, pie!

i'd seen your friend, um... Mara?
Yeah.
Mara, yes. i'd seen her several times at Usher, and then you were with her one night, so i was curious.
Yeah, Mara's there a lot... so um...
Hey Fern, do you play video games at all?
oh, um... no, not really, why?
Jus' curious, is all. You should come to one of our awesome sleep-overs!
you have awesome sleep-overs?

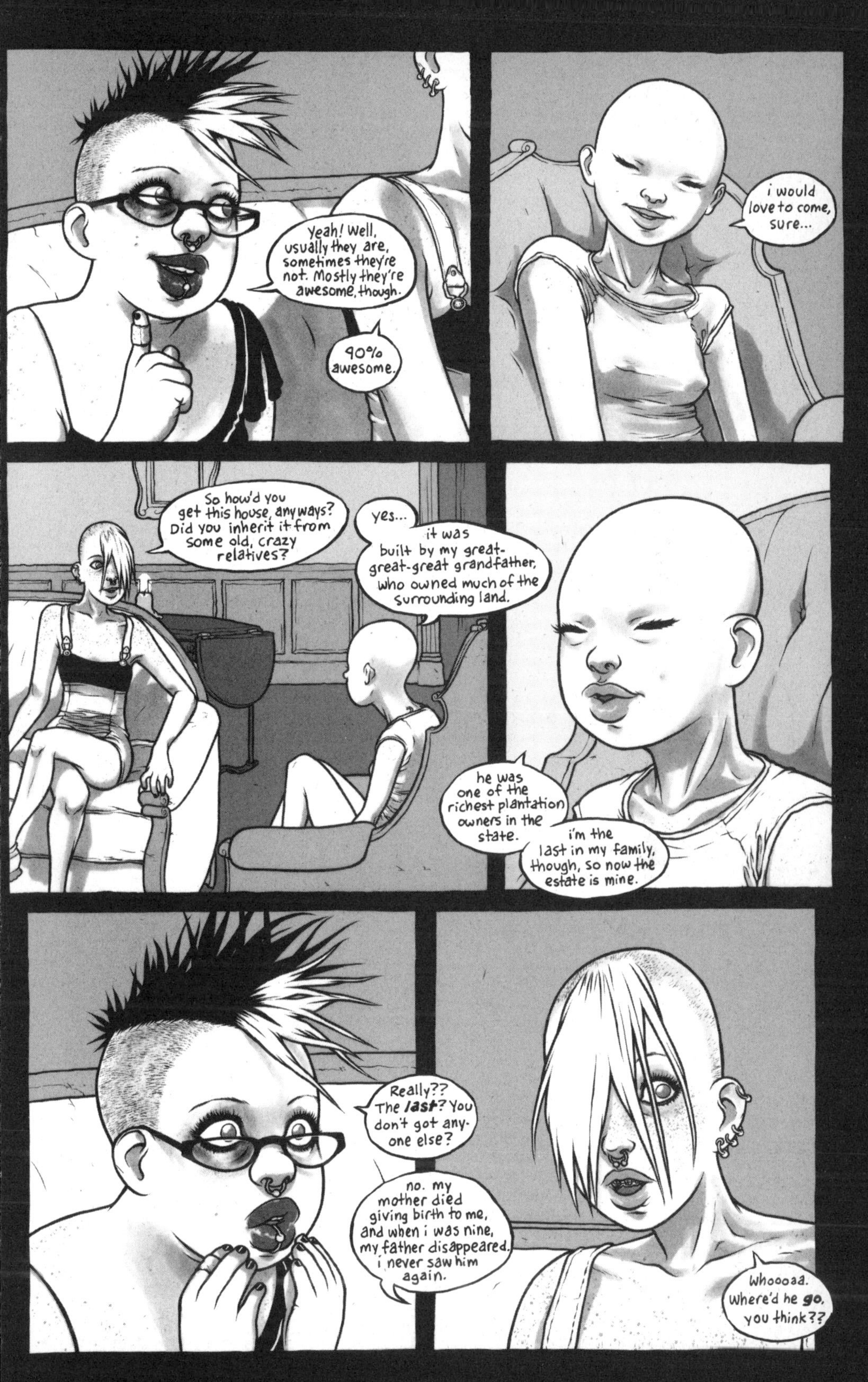
Yeah! Well, usually they are, sometimes they're not. Mostly they're awesome, though.
90% awesome.
i would love to come, sure...
So how'd you get this house, anyways? Did you inherit it from some old, crazy relatives?
yes...
it was built by my great-great-great grandfather, who owned much of the surrounding land.
he was one of the richest plantation owners in the state.
i'm the last in my family, though, so now the estate is mine.
Really?? The **last**? You don't got any-one else?
no. my mother died giving birth to me, and when i was nine, my father disappeared. i never saw him again.
Whoooaa. Where'd he **go**, you think??

i don't know... i hope someday he'll surprise me with his return.
Whoa... so you're here all alone, all the time, then?
well, i have Glaucus, my chef Olivia, and my maid Clementine... i also have a part time gardener, Sam, who's very attractive.
Ooh, a hot gardener, that's what I need!
Yeah, me too. I could definitely use a hot gardener.

Thanks for nothin', you guys.
Hey, we tried, okay?!
Yeah, Penny... there was jus' nothin' to find!
Yeah, like... evidence of purse-snoopin'? What would there even be?
Well, I don't know!
I knew we wouldn't find nothin', I jus' wanted to find secret passages.

FRANKENSTEIN

I wasn't... I ain't sittin' on that thing.

What a lame visit to Fern's. No evidence, no secret passages, no Fern in a weird, hot, vinyl outfit...

CURVE

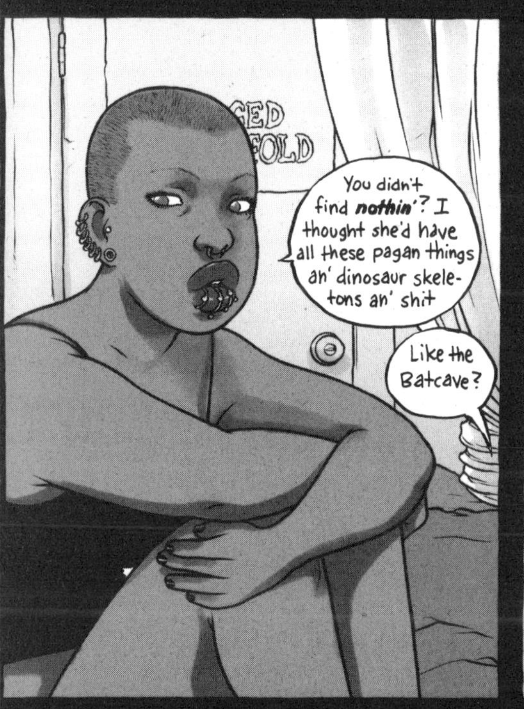

That sounds cool.
Ew.
She wasn't wearin' one a her hot bondage things, though? What'd she got on?
Like, a normal outfit... t-shirt, cut-offs...
She looks good in any-thing.
'Cept for her fucked up mutant arm.
Mara!
What? It's true, she's jus' inbred or some-thin', it ain't her fault.
Well, I happen to **like** her little arm! It's **cute**.
Yeah, c'mon Mara, lay off.
Whatever... I guess it's kinda cute.

VAGINAL
BLOOD
FART

Why you think it was Myrtle?
Well... I'm not positive, but... I told her the story, so... who else could know?
It's totally Myrtle.
It better be. I'll be so mad if it turns out to be Vincent.
God, I know! I'll be madder than you!
What?! C'mon, I'll be, like, the maddest, you ain't even close. I'll be so mad I'll even punch Cleo an' knock her out so Vincent can't have her.
What're you talkin' about? You think that'll stop him? You'd be makin' it easier! Cleo unconscious? Pft! Less trouble for him!
12:23

What? I'm what?
Nothin,' hon, we was jus' talkin' about, um, about Myrtle.
What about her?
Nothin.' Where's that pie you said Malady brought home?
You said it was non-dairy?
Yeah, that's what she said...it's in the fridge on the top shelf.
Cool. Audrey, you want some?
You **sure** it's non-dairy? No eggs, either?
Aren't eggs dairy, too?
No, dummy, eggs are from **chickens**.
No, I know **that**...but, like, I thought they went under dairy...
Dairy's jus' milk stuff.
MY DYING BRIDE
Y'all want some a that pie, then?
No.
Yeah, could you bring me a piece?

So, uh... what the hell'd you tell Cleo?
Huh?
DIMMU BORGIR
'Bout that night we went to Usher...
Nothin', why...?
Au contraire. I managed to discover from a nameless source that **you** said Cleo an' I **did** it.
So...?
I, um... who told you that...?
Guess.
...Cleo?
Duh.
Well, I... I didn't! I didn't say that! I jus' told her what... what you told **me**!
That's not what **she** said. **She** said that you said we **did it**. **Sex** of some kind.
Okay, okay! That's what I thought you **meant**, okay?? I'm sorry, I was– I was confused! I really thought, like– I thought that's what you meant!!

Yeah, well, I guess next time I'll be a little clearer, huh? Oh, wait! There won't be a next time, Big Mouth!
What??
Trilby, come on! I wasn't tryin' to blab or nothin', I didn't mean it! I didn't know it was a big deal!
Whatever. I'm surprised Mara hasn't said anything, since I'm sure she knows, too.
I didn't say nothin' to her!
Should I expect Slicer to crack jokes about it next time I come over?
No! Come on!
NO

So when they were born, all their guts an' shit were all hangin' out, like the skin wasn't strong enough to hold all their intestines in.
So the twins came out all mutilated.
Eww!
Yeah. They did all this surgery on 'em, since like, they obviously couldn't live with all their guts fallin' out.
So yeah, they lived, but I guess they got all these problems now, like, Mrs. LeMare was sayin' one of 'em's like, fuckin' retarded, an' the other one's sick all the time.
Sephen Shock
THISMEANSYOU
Wow...
The retard one's a garbage man, an' he wrecks people's mailboxes on purpose.
I wish Marissa was born all mutilated like that.
She'd still be with Ben, though.

No way, 'cause she'd have some big, nasty scar down her midsection, revolting any one who saw it.
So, yesterday, I chucked this mushy orange I got from the one-arm girl at the coffee shop at Marissa, an' then I hid behind a tree.
The orange only splattered a little on her leg, but it was still pretty funny.
Why'd that girl give you a gross orange?
She had it on the counter with her, an' I asked if I could have it.
You should really, like... give up on Ben an' Marissa, hon... it's crazy...
Look who's fuckin' **talking**.
At least I'm ***trying*** to move on, okay? I think I'm doin' a pretty good job, too!

Yeah...
So, I was outside last night, an' there's this fluffy orange cat that lives here...
I dunno how he got up here, but he **bit** me, look... Bad kitty.
whoa, really?
Yeah! He looked nice at first, but then he bit me an' ran away.
Maybe he smelled meiko on me.
Maybe he drinks blood.
Cats don't drink blood!
What about bird blood? Cats eat birds. Mice, too.
Hm, yeah... maybe... he didn't drink from my finger, he jus' bit it real quick.
Maybe it was a warnin' bite. Maybe you're in his territory, an' he'll terrorize you 'til you leave.
God... I sure hope not...

Or maybe he jus' lives here, or belongs to somebody here.
You can't have pets here, though.
Doesn't mean nobody didn't bring him anyways.
KNOK KNOK
it's the item-dropper! shh! shh!
how d'you know?? what if it's not??
say "who is it"!
no, just open it!!

do it!
careful!

clik

oh...!

Myrtle—
what...
what're you
doin'...?

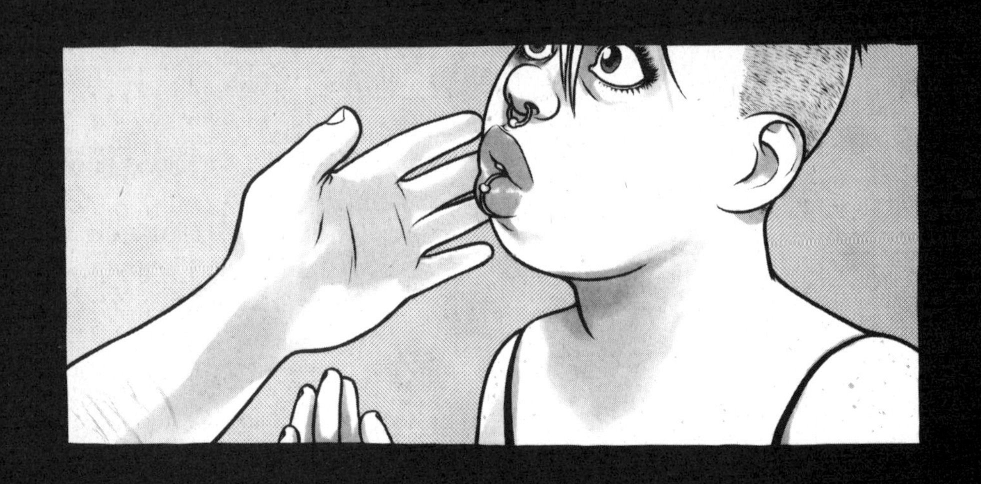

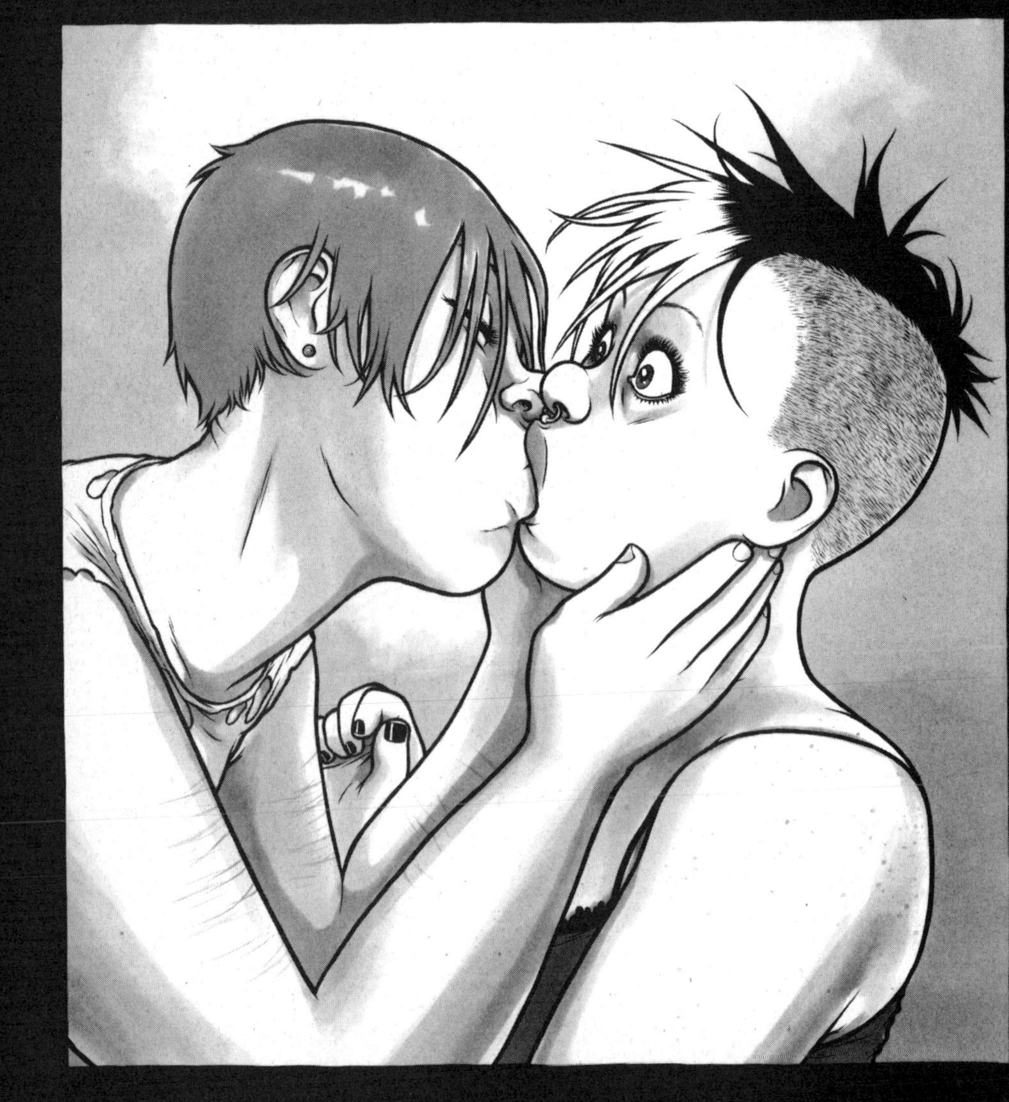

NEXT:

Beth vs. Kinzoku!

Trilby vs. Connor!

Bella Morte vs. the Slutty Angels!

Cleo vs. Kirk Gauthier!

Meiko vs. the Mystery Cat!

Mara vs. Herself!

Myrtle by
Darrin Perry

Natalie by
Natalia Pierandrei

Cleo by Kate Dolamore

Cleo by
Sybaria M. Sybaris

who's who in wet moon

cleo lovedrop

penny lovedrop

trilby bernarde

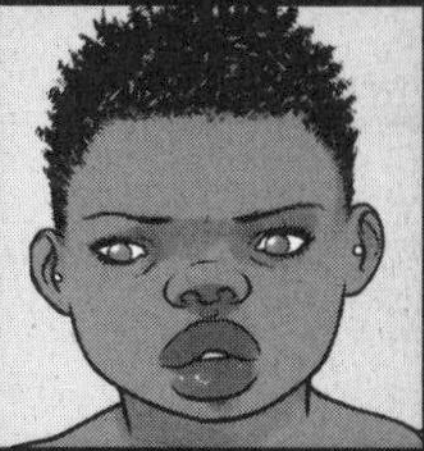
audrey richter

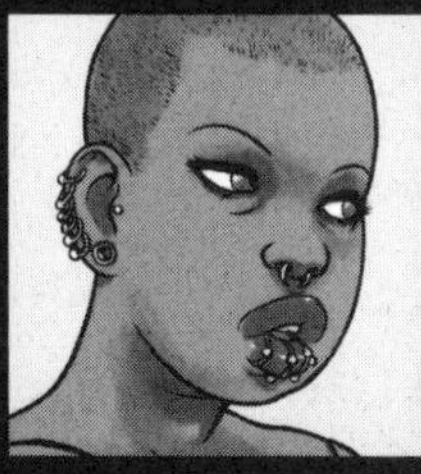
mara zuzanny

myrtle turenne

martin samson

glen neuhoff

fern

natalie ringtree

malady mayapple

beth mckenzie

kinzoku

meiko

?

fall swanhilde

marissa lyons

ben viola

vincent verrier

zia morlon

Special thanks to: Mom, Dad, Julie, James, Joe, Jess, Becky C., Zach, Dan, Gwen, Nate, Tracy, Brandon G., the Bella Morte guys (Andy, Gopal, Tony, Micah & Jordan), Autumn's Grey Solace, Jamaica, Kirk, Nam, and everyone at deviantart.

No thanks to: Bill Goodin, Desert Pepper Trading Co., those damn attic squirrels, my digestive tract, anything in the 3 square mile radius around my apartment.

Plugs: bellamorte.com, autumnsgreysolace.com, thelastdance.com, thismeansyou.com, intenebris.com, cadaveria.com, nateandsteve.com, ridingshotgun.com, jamaicad.com, brothersgraham.com, dpdagger.deviantart.com

Ross Campbell is an art monk who currently lives in Rochester, New York. His first published work was for White Wolf Publishing's *Exalted* RPG books, which he continues to do illustrations for today. He made his comics debut doing the flashbacks in *Too Much Hopeless Savages* and then illustrated *Spooked* (written by Antony Johnston), both published by Oni Press. The first volume of *Wet Moon* was released in 2005, also published by Oni, followed by *The Abandoned* published by Tokyopop. He spends his time working and not much else, but he gets some time off to watch a movie or two every Friday. His personal website is www.greenoblivion.com, and his deviantArt gallery is at mooncalfe.deviantart.com.